ANCIENT EGYPTIAN RELIGION

ANCIENT EGYPTIAN
RELIGION

by

JAROSLAV ČERNÝ

PROFESSOR OF EGYPTOLOGY IN THE UNIVERSITY OF OXFORD, SOMETIME
EDWARDS PROFESSOR OF EGYPTOLOGY, UNIVERSITY COLLEGE, LONDON

GREENWOOD PRESS, PUBLISHERS
WESTPORT, CONNECTICUT

Library of Congress Cataloging in Publication Data

Černý, Jaroslav, paleographer.
  Ancient Egyptian religion.

  Reprint of the 1957 printing of the work originally
published in 1952 by Hutchinson's University Library,
London, in series: Hutchinson's university library,
World religions.
  Bibliography: p.
  Includes index.
  1. Egypt--Religion. I. Title.
[BL2441.2.C47 1979]   299'.31   78-9931
ISBN 0-313-21104-3

First published 1952
Reprinted 1957

Reprinted with the permission of Hutchinson Publishing
Group Limited.

Reprinted in 1979 by Greenwood Press, Inc.,
51 Riverside Avenue, Westport, CT 06880

Printed in the United States of America

10 9 8 7 6 5 4 3 2

CONTENTS

v

PREFACE

I CONSENTED to write this sketch of the ancient Egyptian religion only after it had become clear that this task would not be undertaken by any of the persons possessing more competent knowledge of the subject than I did then or do now. It was at a time when I was not fully aware of the extent of my future duties; these were responsible for the considerable delay in the publication of the book.

Egyptologists who might choose to read it will certainly not be satisfied. It is not for them, however, that the book has been planned and written, but rather for the inquiring layman. The limited space available made it imperative to be brief and to include only what is really important. I cannot claim originality for any of my statements; what the general reader needs is rather a condensation of the results of research which are mostly to be found in special publications inaccessible to him and written in part in languages with which he is not acquainted. The times when books on Egyptian religion consisted of illustrated catalogues of strange Egyptian gods are happily over and so are the days when the Egyptian religion was presented as a mere aspect of the political history of the country. This change has increased the difficulty of dealing with the Egyptian religion in a simple and understandable style. The aim of this small book will be fulfilled if the intelligent reader finds in it the answers to his questions and becomes interested enough to follow up the subject by reading some of the books listed in the bibliography at the end of the volume.

JAROSLAV ČERNÝ.

London,
University College,
1951.

vii

CHRONOLOGICAL TABLE

Prehistoric Period (before 3200 B.C.).

Badarian, Tasian, Nagadean Periods; "Scorpion" King.

Protodynastic Period (3200–2800 B.C.).

Ist Dynasty:
    Menes (=Narmer?); Djer; Djet; Udymu; Merpabia.
IInd Dynasty:
    Nebrē, Peribsen.

Old Kingdom (2800–2250 B.C.).

IIIrd Dynasty (2800–2740 B.C.).
    Khasekhemui; Djoser.
IVth Dynasty (2740–2580 B.C.).
    Cheops (Khufu).
    Djedefrē.
    Chefren (Khafrē).
    Mykerinos (Menkaurē).
Vth Dynasty (2580–2440 B.C.).
    Sahurē.
    Neuserrē.
    Djedkerē.
    Unis.
VIth Dynasty (2440–2250 B.C.).

First Intermediate Period (2250–2000 B.C.).

VIIth—Xth Dynasties.
XIth Dynasty.
    Intef I.

Middle Kingdom (2000–1780 B.C.).

XIIth Dynasty.
    Amenemhēt I.
    Senwosret III.

Second Intermediate Period, including Hyksos Period
(1780–1546 B.C.).

XIIIth–XVIIth Dynasties.

New Kingdom (1546–1085 B.C.).
XVIIIth Dynasty (1546–1319 B.C.).
    Amenhotep I (1546–1525).
    Tuthmosis I (1525–1508).
    Queen Hatshepsut (1504–1482).
    Tuthmosis III (1482–1450).
    Amenhotep II (1450–1425).
    Tuthmosis IV (1425–1412).
    Amenhotep III (1412–1375).
    Amenhotep IV—Ekhnaton (1387–1366).
    Tutankhaton (later Tutankhamun, 1366–1357).
    Haremhab (1353–1319).
XIXth Dynasty (1318–1200).
    Sethos I (1318–1299).
    Ramesses II (1299–1232).
XXth Dynasty (1200–1085).
    Ramesses III (1198–1167).
    Ramesses IV (1167–1161).
Late Periods (1085–525 B.C.).
XXVth Dynasty (Ethiopian Period) (712–661 B.C.).
    Shabaka (712–700).
    Tanutamun (663–661).
XXVIth (Saite) Dynasty (663–525).
    Psammetichus I (663–609).
    Amasis (569–526).
Persian Period (525–332 B.C.).
    Darius I (521–486).
Graeco-Roman Period (332 B.C.–A.D. 640).
    Alexander the Great (332–323).
Ptolemaic Rule (323–30 B.C.).
    Ptolemy I Soter I (323–285).
    Ptolemy II Philadelphus (285–246).
    Ptolemy III Euergetes I (246–222).
    Ptolemy IV Philopator (222–203).
    Ptolemy V Epiphanes (203–181).
    Ptolemy VI Philometor (181–146).
    Ptolemy IX Euergetes II (146–117).
    Ptolemy XI Alexander I (106–88).
    Ptolemy XIII Neos Dionysos (Auletes) (80–51).
    Cleopatra (51–30) with Ptolemy XVI Caesarion (45–44).

Roman Rule (30 B.C.–A.D. 395).
    Augustus (30 B.C.–A.D. 14).
    Tiberius (14–37).
    Caligula (37–41).
    Vespasian (69–79).
    Domitian (81–96).
    Hadrian (117–138).
    Marcus Aurelius (161–180).
    Caracalla (211–217).
    Decius (249–251).
    Gallienus (260–268).
    Diocletian (284–305).
    Constantine the Great (324–337).
    Constantius (337–361).
    Theodosius the Great (379–395).
Byzantine Rule (A.D. 395–640).
    Marcian (450–457).
    Justinian (527–565).

CHAPTER I

INTRODUCTION

THE course of time over which religion, its changes and its
development can be observed within the limits of one and the
same civilization is unusually long in Egypt, since the period
under observation extends from the oldest written records,
dating from about 3200 B.C., down to the final victory of
Christianity in the third century A.D. As early as the beginning
of this period Egyptian religion had assumed a developed and
complex character, though it still contained many relics of the
earlier stages through which it had passed in the preceding
prehistoric age.

Religion, being inspired by the emotions, can only be ade-
quately revealed in writing, while the other witnesses of human
thought, the products of material culture, seldom admit of
exact and incontestable interpretation as to their bearing upon
the realm of religious beliefs.

No conclusion concerning the religion of palaeolithic man
in Egypt can be formed, since from that remote period of prehistory nothing has come down to us except crude flint implements found either *in situ* on the high desert plateau on both
sides of the Nile or washed down into the Nile Valley by rain-
fall. The Libyan desert in the west and the Arabian desert in
the east were at that time covered with vegetation and inhabited
by men and beasts, but towards the end of the palaeolithic period
desiccation had progressed so far that living creatures were
forced to retreat into the swampy Nile Valley along the whole
of its long course. There we find men settled in numerous
communities at the points where they had reached the river,
at the beginning of the neolithic period. Agriculture was already
practised but hunting game, which was abundant, was still an
important, if not the main, method of providing food. The early
formation of communities seems to be best explained by the
special character of the Nile Valley. Its soil was rich but needed

irrigation by canals and protection by dykes; both canals and dykes could only be constructed by the combined efforts of an organized community.

Both Upper and Lower Egypt were inhabited in the neolithic period, though only the former has so far been explored by archaeologists, the remains in Lower Egypt being now buried deep under the mud since brought down by the Nile. Three main stages or cultures are differentiated in Upper Egypt and are called respectively Tasian, Badarian and Nagadean, their names being derived from the modern villages of Der Tasa, Badari and Nagada at which their traces were first identified. All three differ not only in age, but also in forms of pottery and implements. The settlement at Merimde Benisalame in Lower Egypt seems to be contemporaneous with the Tasian, though its culture appears to be entirely different. On the other hand, the finds at the Lower Egyptian site of Maadi, which are contemporaneous with the middle or the latest stage at Nagada, seem to suggest that by that time the two parts of the country shared a common material culture.

The main evidence of religious beliefs in the neolithic period is derived from tombs, for cemeteries representing the above-mentioned cultures have been found. Vessels containing food and drink, tools, arms and primitive jewellery were placed in these graves and their very occurrence is a clear proof that they were thought to be indispensable to the dead. Consequently, a belief must have prevailed in an existence after death, and this existence was imagined to be very similar to the earthly life. No effort was made to preserve the body, this task being left to the natural dryness of the desert sand and the Egyptian climate. At Badari corpses were often wrapped in skins which were probably the common clothing of the hunter of that time; clothing therefore was also thought to be of importance for the dead. To prevent the bodies from being dug up by wild animals they were placed under mats, under large pots (at the close of the prehistoric period), in wooden cases or in coffins.

At Merimde-Benisalame the dead were not buried in cemeteries but within the settlement, sometimes actually inside the houses of the inhabitants, near the fireplace; this may indicate no more than that they were thought to need the warmth of the fire, but perhaps also that they went on forming part of the community and participating in its life. At Badari the earliest tombs are not far from the village, but later ones are grouped in separate cemeteries sometimes at a considerable distance; the after-life of the dead, therefore, was then thought to be less closely connected with that of the living.

It is more difficult to explain the attitude in which dead bodies almost invariably appear in the neolithic period. This is the same more or less tightly contracted position found at that period all over Europe, North Africa and Western Asia, and showing the body with curved spine and legs bent so that the thighs sometimes nearly touch the body, while the hands are placed in front of the face. Various explanations have been suggested by prehistorians. It is probable that the intention of saving space and making the graves smaller, and thus less laborious to dig with primitive tools, played a less important part than the intention of placing the body in the most natural position for sleep. If the second explanation be correct, another important feature of the ancient conception of death would be revealed: death would have been imagined as a kind of rest or sleep, something to be desired by primitive man who was occupied with hard work during all his life. It is clear that the process of contraction could only have been achieved soon after death and it is even possible that the early Egyptians practised the same custom as a modern African tribe who bend the bodies of their dead in a very similar manner at the approach of death. This explanation may also account for the sporadic occurrence of stretched-out bodies in prehistoric times: they would belong to people discovered too long after death when contraction was no longer practicable.

The normal position of the body lying in the grave was on the left side; such is the case at Badari, throughout the Nagada period, under the first dynasties and as late as the Middle Kingdom. In the Pyramid texts it was also assumed that the dead king was lying on his left side for he was summoned to rise and turn over from his left to his right side to receive offerings. Nevertheless, at Merimde-Benisalame the majority of the bodies were placed on the right side and at el-Amrah, in Upper Egypt, the same position is general.

The position of tombs was with the longer axis running from north to south, local north being the direction in which the Nile flows at any particular place. The head was placed towards the south so that the body faced west. At Merimde-Benisalame however the tombs were mostly placed so that the dead faced north or north-east, while at el-Amrah they faced east; the same rule applied also to many of the tombs at Gerzeh (middle of the Nagada period), and particularly at Turah (towards the end of the prehistoric period).

The question whether any importance is to be attributed to the side on which the body lay and the direction which it faced raises a problem. Does it imply any change in the beliefs concerning the life after death if the dead face north or east instead of west? In the historical period the place where the dead go is supposed to be in the west; the mysterious and endless desert where the sun sets suggested to the mind of the ancient Egyptians an imaginary dwelling place of the dead, while the eastern desert must have been crossed in very early times and found to end at the Red Sea. But the east is the quarter in which the sun rises every morning and by watching its daily reappearance the dead might have expected a renewal of life. The practice of lying the body with its head pointing north may be accounted for by the fact, known from certain old religious texts, that the souls of the dead were believed to live among the stars of the northern sky which may be only a survival of the belief current in the Merimde-Benisalame period.

On decorated vases of about the middle of the Nagada period there are painted representations of what are now generally believed to be boats with cabins on deck. Their purpose is not quite clear; perhaps they represent funerary vessels crossing the river. On the roof of the cabin there is a high pole—less frequently a pair—on top of which is mounted an object or an animal. About midway up the pole are two oblique strokes which are clearly meant to represent ribbons fluttering in the air. A small number of the objects and animals can be identified without difficulty: a palm-branch, two, three or four mountains,

the sun, and an object resembling the cult sign later characteristic of the god Min, an elephant, a bird, a goat or a gazelle are
all easy to recognize. The majority, however, are drawn too
crudely to be identified with any degree of probability. A total
of two dozen different objects has hitherto been noted.

In all probability these standards represent the ensigns of
prehistoric Egyptian deities, since they closely resemble the
divine ensigns of the historical period when the cult-object or
animal is similarly placed on a high pole and adorned with two
ribbons. It seems reasonable to conclude that the boats
flew the ensigns of their local gods as the distinguishing
mark of their native port. The variety of prehistoric deities
is quite consistent with what is known of conditions in historical
times, and the fact that many prehistoric ensigns do not recur
later cannot be adduced as a serious objection to this interpretation: local gods often fell into oblivion, being overshadowed
by their rivals from more flourishing localities.

Archaeological evidence, though invaluable for the study of
material culture in prehistoric Egypt, offers, therefore, little
guidance to the student of its religion. Very little precise information can be gleaned concerning funerary ideas and nothing
is known about the gods of that time except that they were
many and that their cult-objects and animals had already been
assigned. Of the gods found in later times only Min of Koptos
can be identified with some degree of probability from his cult-
object on the vases and on one carved slate palette used for
preparing eye-paint which was found in a tomb at el-Amrah
dating from the middle of the Nagada period. It is, however,
clear that animal worship in some form dates back to remote
antiquity, since cemeteries of jackals, bulls, rams and gazelles,
carefully wrapped in mats or linen, have been found which date
from the Badarian civilization.

A series of large ceremonial palettes and mace-heads dating
from the close of the prehistoric and the beginning of the dynastic ages show in relief representations of historical or semi-
historical events; included in these scenes are clear examples
of portable ensigns, which occupy a significant place in the
whole composition. On a palette showing a lion-hunt two
ensigns with falcons and a third with an almond-shaped object

are carried by hunters. On another palette depicting a battle-field covered with corpses and birds of prey, two ensigns sur-mounted by a falcon and an ibis are each provided with an arm holding a prisoner of the same race as the corpses lying on the battlefield; and on a fragment of yet another palette recording the destruction of some towns, five ensigns, two bearing jackals (or dogs), and the remainder bearing an ibis, a falcon and the cult-object of Min, terminate in hands holding a rope. Although the object tied to each rope is now broken away, it was surely a prisoner. On a large mace-head of the king "Scorpion" these standards, to which bows and strangled birds are attached, are included in an agricultural ceremony while other emblems are carried before the king. An identical series of four standards, with a jackal (or dog), a curious oval object (similar to the later emblem of the Theban god Khons) and two falcons, is carried in front of the king on a mace-head and a palette of King Narmer. This king is probably identical with Menes of later tradition and thus the scenes on the palette are perhaps a con-temporary record of the unification of Upper and Lower Egypt under a single ruler.

The same standards accompanying the king are often shown in representations of festivals in historical times, and even Clement of Alexandria (writing in the third century A.D.) relates that the Egyptians in the festival processions of their gods still "carried about golden images, two dogs, one hawk and one ibis". The inscriptions which sometimes accompany these standards on Egyptian reliefs specifically identify them with certain gods; they are, therefore, emblems of deities which the early Egyptians carried when they went hunting or advanced into battle as well as in their festivals.

A similar kind of standard was used in historic times in writing the names of the administrative districts into which Egypt was divided. These districts were called *nomoi* ("sections") by the Greeks; their number varied slightly from time to time; the traditional number in later nome-lists was twenty-two for Upper Egypt and twenty for Lower Egypt. The nomes were clearly the last remnants of the small independent city-states of the prehistoric age which had gradually coalesced or had been forcibly welded into the two kingdoms of Upper and

Lower Egypt. The Greek names of particular nomes were derived from the later capitals of each district (*e.g.*, Lykopolites [nomos], [the nome] of Lykonpolis, the original Egyptian name of which was Siowtey), but in Egyptian hieroglyphic writing the names of nomes are nearly always written with standards, the earliest certain example being the name of the XVth Upper Egyptian nome from the time of Djoser, the first king of the IIIrd Dynasty.

Political and religious individualism went hand in hand in prehistoric times; each locality had its own deity, bearing its own name and manifested in some animal or object. We can therefore say that Egyptian religion in the earliest stage known to us was fetishistic. The local deity was the "town-god" and as such he figures in inscriptions as the highest authority recognized by the inhabitants; he was the "lord" of the town. If the number of these local deities decreased with the passage of time, when certain of them were largely forgotten, it was certainly due to the fact that the gods of those localities which were more important politically and economically overshadowed or absorbed the gods of the less important places. In other cases two deities were so similar in character that they merged into one.

As a consequence of the use of a pole with two attached ribbons to bear the early emblems of the god, the Egyptians adopted this symbol, when writing was invented, to express the general idea of "god" and "divine". The later forms of the sign resemble very closely an axe and used to be so regarded by Egyptologists, but carefully executed and coloured examples of the sign have revealed its true nature; indeed, the early dynastic form of the sign clearly shows the two ribbons projecting horizontally from the pole, while in the predynastic representations of divine emblems they slope obliquely or hang down vertically. The hieroglyphic sign in question was read *nutjer* which is preserved in Coptic as *nute* and is the word used to express the idea of the Christian God when the New Testament was being translated into Coptic in the early centuries of our era.

Some account of the chief deities represented by fetishes must now be given; we shall include all those occurring on the monuments of the first three dynasties, and also some which appear only in later records, the inference being that their absence from earlier writings is the result of chance. The prominence given to deities of Upper Egypt is due to our lack of information about the religion of Lower Egypt in early times. The order followed is not geographical but deities are grouped according to the character of their cult animal or object.

It is seldom that actual images of animals or the objects sacred to particular deities are found; in most cases their existence must be inferred from the use of their pictures as signs in writing the names of the gods in question. Some animals are represented as living, while others are put on pedestals, provided with sceptres, crowns or feathers, or stylized in various ways, and were consequently considered as idols made of stone, wood, clay or metal. Statues of gods, therefore, must have existed even in this remote period; the making of such a statue is known to have been an important event, because in the annals of the first three dynasties the regnal years of kings were sometimes so named, e.g., "the year of forming (the statue of) Anubis" under the second king of the Ist Dynasty.

Wild animals, though eagerly hunted, were regarded with special awe and respect because of their great strength and ferocity; and the lion and wild bull appear on the palettes of the late prehistoric period and on the palette of Narmer as symbols of the victorious deified king trampling on his defeated enemies. It is the lioness rather than the lion that appears as an actual deity bearing various names. She is found as Matit in the XIIth nome of Upper Egypt (first encountered in the tombs of the Old Kingdom at Der el-Gebrawi), as Mehit at This in the VIIIth nome, whose worship can be traced back to the Ist Dynasty, and as Pekhet at Speos Artemidos in the XVth nome, where, however, her cult is not attested before the Middle Kingdom.

The worship of the wild bull can only be surmised from the standards of several nomes of Lower Egypt and that of the hippopotamus is so far known only from a relatively late period (the New Kingdom). A crocodile cult existed at various places all over the country, notably at Gebelen, Denderah and Sais, and later also in the Fayyum. The name of the crocodile-god was Subek (Greek Suchos).

Numerous small statuettes of baboons and a representation of this animal on an ivory label suggest that its cult dates from the beginning of Egyptian history; it may have been practised at Khmun (Hermopolis), where presumably it preceded the cult of the ibis of Thoth. The original reading of the name of this baboon god is uncertain; but later he was called Hedj-wer or Hedjwerew and interpreted as the "Great White One" or "Whitest of the Great Ones".

The cult animal of Sētekh in the representations on the gravestones of the Ist Dynasty somewhat resembles a donkey. It has relatively long legs, long and broad ears and a short upright tail. It seems, however, that at an early date, at least by the Old Kingdom, the Egyptians transformed it into a fabulous animal, usually depicted as a recumbent dog, with a long neck and an upright tail, squared ears and a long, curved muzzle. It is then not surprising that the efforts of Egypto-logists to identify this creature with an actual animal have been unsuccessful.

The cradle of Sētekh was Enboyet (Greek Ombos), a town in the Vth nome of Upper Egypt, between the modern villages of Nagada and Ballas. It has been supposed that the time of Enboyet's greatest prosperity was shortly before the beginning of the dynastic period and the extensive cemeteries of that time situated in its neighbourhood support this view. With the foundation of the Ist Dynasty the cult of Sētekh spread far beyond the limits of the Vth nome: Sētekh became "Lord of Upper Egypt" and a representative god of the whole of that part of the country. In that capacity he became a dangerous rival to Horus and this rivalry shaped the conception of the nature of the god and his subsequent destiny, which will be described later in the present chapter.

In the XVIth nome of Upper Egypt the worship of the oryx-antelope is attested by the occurrence of that animal as the nome-sign, an example of which can be quoted from the time of Djoser. The cult of the animal was very early superseded by that of the falcon of Horus.

The dog was domesticated by the Egyptians at a very remote period. Probably on account of his usefulness in the chase, Canidae of various kinds were chosen in many places as cult-animals, the different species not being clearly distinguished in representations. One of the most common canine deities was Upuaut, "the way-opener", the god of Siut, who betrays his role of scout by his very name. This was originally perhaps only an epithet, the true name of the god being Sed, who occurs very early and whose standard has exactly the same appearance as that of Upuaut. Upuaut was the god whose ensign was carried in front of the king into battle and during victory celebrations from late prehistoric times onwards. As the Greek name of Siut, Lykonpolis shows, the Greeks identified the animal of Upuaut with the wolf; more probably it may have been a wild dog and it is as a dog that Clement of Alexandria describes Upuaut's ensign.

A true dog is represented in Anupew, better known under the Greek form of his name, Anubis, whose cult was practised at several places in the XVIIth nome of Upper Egypt, the capital of which bore in Greek times the name of Kynopolis, *i.e.*, "town of dogs". The animal of Anubis is always represented lying down, often with an ostrich feather on his back. From time immemorial he was a god of the dead and protector of burials; the dog was an animal who disturbed tombs while searching for bones, his cult, therefore, was a kind of *captatio benevolentiae*.

Another recumbent dog connected with the dead was Khenti-Amentiu, "Foremost of the Westerners", as his name shows; he was the original god of Abydos, but later became merged into Osiris. Yet another dog-(or jackal-) god in mummified form is attested early in the IVth Dynasty, but both his name and the seat of his worship are unknown.

The cat- or mongoose-goddess Mafdet, "lady of the Castle of Life", attested from the Ist Dynasty, was very early invoked as a protectress against snake bites, as both Egyptian cats and mongooses were fearless snake-killers. The centre of the cult of this goddess is still unknown.

The vulture-goddess Nekhbet, whose original home was at Enkhab (modern El-Kab) in the IIIrd nome of Upper Egypt, seems to have no distinctive name, for Nekhbet means only "She of Enkhab". In the predynastic period she became the tutelary goddess of the Upper Egyptian kingdom. The other important vulture-goddess, Mut of Ioshrew—a part of Thebes —does not come into any prominence before the Middle Kingdom.

Another cult which figures in the predynastic period is that of the falcon of Horus (Egyptian Horew, "Lofty One"), a suitable name for a high-flying bird of prey. He was worshipped in many localities, to which he came from his most important centre at Hierakonpolis (Egyptian, Nekhen) in the IIIrd nome of Upper Egypt, the capital of the predynastic kingdom of Upper Egypt. Whether this was his original place of worship, however, is not quite certain; opinions of scholars are divided on this matter, some preferring to regard Behdet in the Delta as his earliest home. At least as early as the beginning of the historical period Horus was well established at Hierakonpolis and was there identified with the king of Upper Egypt, who was consequently known as Horus. Horus was a sky-god and as early as the Ist Dynasty he is represented in a boat crossing the sky.

Another town with an important cult of Horus lay in Upper Egypt and was known as Behdet (now Edfu), after which Horus was often called Behdety, "He of Behdet", and various falcon-gods elsewhere in Egypt were later identified with Horus, *e.g.*, Khentekhtay at Athribis in Lower Egypt, who is only attested at a relatively late period. Instances in Upper Egypt are the falcon-god of the town of Hebenu (now Zawiet el-Meitin) in the XVIth nome and the god of the XIIIth nome. A "northern Horus" is mentioned in the IVth Dynasty, being so called probably to distinguish him from the original Horus of Hierakonpolis. Pairs of falcons were worshipped in the Vth Upper Egyptian nome of Koptos and the Xth of Aphroditopolis.

The cult of the ibis (*Ibis religiosa*) is found as early as the Ist Dynasty and is connected with the god Thoth. The origin of the name and his earliest place of worship are unknown. His standard appears on the palettes of the predynastic period, which suggests that he was an Upper Egyptian deity, but it was only in the Middle Kingdom that he received the title of

"Lord of Khmun" after the town of Khmun (Greek Hermo-polis, now Ashmunein) which both then and later was the most important centre of his worship.

Among serpents the dangerous cobra was the animal of the goddess Wedjoyet, "The Green One", of Buto in the VIth nome of Lower Egypt. She became the tutelary goddess of the Lower Egyptian kingdom, the capital of which was Buto, and retained this role after the unification of the two lands.

The reproductive processes of the frog were a mystery to the ancient Egyptians which explains why a goddess, Heket, assumed the form of a frog; at least as early as the IVth Dynasty she was worshipped at Antinoupolis (Egn. Hiwōr) in the XVIth nome of Upper Egypt.

It is curious that in comparison with numerous cults of quadrupeds and birds those of fish were relatively rare. Still, a fish-god Neres or Neser is known under the first dynasties and the ensign of the XVIth nome of Lower Egypt, which displays the image of a dolphin, proves that the cult of a fish-goddess, called Hatmehit, existed there from the time of the Middle Kingdom.

Domestic animals as a class are represented in many different cults; bulls and rams impressed the peasant folk by their reproductive power, and cows by their motherly care. The cult of the bull Hapi (Greek Apis) at Memphis goes back to at least as early as the Ist Dynasty, that of Merwer (Greek Mnevis) at Heliopolis is probably as old, although it is not attested until later. We know little more than the names of other sacred bulls, all presumably from Lower Egypt: "white bull", "great black (bull)", "great bull" and "anointed bull". They all appear in the Old Kingdom and they must have received varying degrees of worship, since, while the two last mentioned had their own "priests" ("servants of the god"), the "white bull" and the Apis had only a "staff", i.e., "keeper". The "great black (bull)" is the god of the Xth Lower Egyptian nome. Cow goddesses were worshipped in several nomes, notably in the VIIth and XXIInd of Upper and the IIIrd of Lower Egypt; they were, however, very early identified with the goddess Hathor of Denderah and it is uncertain which of them—if any—is depicted as human-headed with cow's ears and horns on the palette of Narmer and on ivories from the tombs of the kings Djer and Merpabia of the Ist Dynasty.

Cults of rams are also known from various monuments dating from the Ist Dynasty and a little later the names of the ram-god Khnum of Elephantine (Ist nome of Upper Egypt) and "Ram of Anpet", probably of Mendes (XVIth Lower Egyptian nome) are of common occurrence. They are joined by an anonymous ram-god bearing the epithet Harshaf, "He who is on his lake" (Greek Harsaphes) of Herakleopolis Magna in the XXth Upper Egyptian nome. They are all represented as living animals and standing, while the god Kherty, originally from an unimportant locality near Letopolis (IInd nome of Lower Egypt), appears in the form of a mummified ram lying down. All these rams belong to the native Egyptian species of sheep (*Ovis longiceps palaeoaegyptiaca*) with long horizontal and slightly wavy horns, which died out during the Middle Kingdom. The ram, on the other hand, in whose form Amun appears from the Middle Kingdom onwards, is of the new species with curved horns and fat tail (*Ovis platyura aegyptiaca*).

The cat-goddess Bastet, attested since the IInd Dynasty, was so named after her cult-town Bast (Greek Bubastis) in the XVIIIth nome of Lower Egypt, her animal, however, was originally perhaps not the domesticated cat, but a lioness.

Plant cults, even in the earliest period now known, are rare, though there is enough evidence that such cults must once have existed. Two Upper Egyptian nome-standards are decorated with trees on the top, but it is difficult to determine their botanical species. One is perhaps an oleander. Various large isolated trees were considered to be seats of deities; thus a sycamore somewhere near Memphis on the desert fringe of the cultivated land was thought to be occupied by a benevolent goddess. She—and probably other tree deities as well—were already identified with Hathor in the Old Kingdom, who accordingly was given the epithet "Lady of the Sycamore". It was believed that the souls of the dead coming in the form of birds from the necropolis nearby would find under the sycamore water and food shaken down by the goddess dwelling in the tree.

Other plants were connected with certain gods or goddesses

and considered as sacred without being regarded as manifestations of divine beings.

Much larger than the category of plants is that of inanimate objects which were considered as the seat of a deity; in principle all objects connected with a temple or with the king were divine. The cult of objects is a very old feature of Egyptian religion; its high antiquity is revealed by the fact that the true nature of some of them is not only unknown to us, but was evidently unknown even to the ancient Egyptians themselves at a very early date.

At Heliopolis a pillar *yon* gave the town its original name *Yonew* (the later form On is found in the Bible). In the same town there was also a stone *benben* in the form of an obelisk, later considered as a seat of the rising sun. Another pillar called *Djed* consisting of a bundle of truncated stems of an unidentified plant was also a cult object which received offerings and had its own priests. It was early connected with Osiris, though originally it did not represent any individual god. A wooden column with a capital in the form of a papyrus flower surmounted by two feathers was a fetish of the god Ukh of Kusai (near the modern Meir) in the XIVth Upper Egyptian nome. It seems to have been originally no more than an object somehow associated with the local cult of Hathor.

Various sceptres, staffs and other insignia of worldly power were considered as cult objects. The sceptre *sekhem* was a symbol of power and its very name also signified "power". It was a seat of divine might, and sceptres of various gods received worship in temples. Osiris, after the establishment of his cult-centre at Abydos, was also personified by such a *sekhem*-sceptre, the top of which was covered with a golden case bearing a human face and surmounted by two feathers. This case was later represented as a human head in accordance with the belief that it was Osiris's head that was buried at Abydos.

Another sceptre, which belonged to the goddess Iamut, was crooked at the top and twisted at the bottom—in reality a herdsman's stick derived from a remote past—and surmounted by three or four horizontal curved ribs of wood(?) and a feather.

The personification of the king's ceremonial beard, Dua-wer, "Great Matutinal One," can be traced back to the reign of Djet of the Ist Dynasty.

The warlike goddess Neith manifested herself in two arrows crossed over a shield; she is among the oldest deities at present attested. Her worship originated in the town of Sais, capital of the IVth and Vth Lower Egyptian nomes, but after the union of the two kingdoms she became popular in Upper Egypt as well.

A star carried on a pole and surmounted by a curved rib with two upward projections was originally the embodiment of the goddess Seshat. An image of two or three mountains on a standard is the emblem of the god of the Libyan desert, Ha. A queer fetish is that of a god called Imiut, "He who is in his wrappings"; it is a pole with an inflated animal skin bag hanging on it. The god was identified with Anubis, the god of the dead, from the early Middle Kingdom. And last but not least the fetish of the god Min already alluded to as appearing on a palette of the Nagada period. Even in the oldest representations the form of the object varies considerably and its nature remains obscure; at the Nagada period it resembles most closely something carved in wood or bone, not unlike a double-headed arrow or harpoon.

The transition from the conception and representation of gods as animals and inanimate objects to their endowment with human form, that is to anthropomorphization, was the same in Egypt as among other peoples who have attained a certain level of civilization. It was prompted on the one hand by a progressive domination of the animal and material world, and on the other by a diminishing appreciation of purely physical qualities (the physical strength of wild beasts, the high-flying powers of birds of prey) and instincts (motherly care of female animals), or by an increased knowledge of the mysterious life of certain animals. Intellectual qualities came to be valued more highly and these were more developed and manifested in man than in any other being. Gods, to whom a high degree of power and intelligence was attributed, were, therefore, bound to assume human form in the end.

It is clear that the anthropomorphization of gods thus marks the last stage in the process of development, though it did not necessarily affect all deities or appear in all classes of the population at the same time: while the higher and more intellectual classes may have progressed to the anthropomorphic conception of their deities, while the more primitive Egyptian peasants still have adhered to the older zoomorphic and fetishistic ideas. Anthropomorphization of gods must have taken place or at least started as early as the prehistoric period. At the beginning of history we find a human-faced deity provided with the horns of a cow, presumably the goddess Hathor, on the slate palette of King Narmer. Three statues of the god Min found at Koptos have generally been ascribed to approximately the same period. It is necessary, however, to stress that this dating was conjectured from their style; the circumstances of their discovery did not allow the excavator to determine their date more precisely than that they preceded Ptolemaic times.

The three statues are represented ithyphallically in human form, naked except for a girdle, with legs joined together and the arms close to the body. The clenched right fist was pierced and may originally have held a whip, the emblem of Min in historic times. The heads of the statues are broken; only one was found, its face sorely mutilated, but with a beard still visible on the cheek. All three statues bear figures of various animals sculptured on the body, among which are fish and shells native to the Red Sea; two statues also show an unidentified object which at all periods served to write the hieroglyphic sign for Min. When complete two of the statues exceeded 4 metres (13 feet) in height.

"Modelling of (a statue of) Min" is recorded under the Ist Dynasty in a fragment of annals, and there, too, Min in writing is represented in human form, this time, however, with the right arm holding the whip raised. The fragment dates from the Vth Dynasty, but the record is probably a faithful copy of a document contemporary with the event.

Under Peribsen of the IInd Dynasty the goddess Wedjoyet is represented on seals with a human face and body and the god Ash is also anthropomorphic, though—if the publications are reliable—his head is sometimes human and sometimes that of a hawk or of the Sētekh-animal. The gods on fragments of reliefs from a temple of Djoser of the IIIrd Dynasty at Heliopolis are all human in form.

The anthropomorphization of gods was undoubtedly influenced to a considerable extent by the identification of the king with the god Horus, an identification which can be demonstrated as dating back at least to the close of the prehistoric period. The falcon of Horus on a standard was used to indicate a deity in hieroglyphic writing during the early part of the Old Kingdom—a clear proof that the Horus-falcon was considered as a god *par excellence*; it was replaced only in the VIth Dynasty by a seated bearded figure. Writing as a rule was rather conservative as this instance shows; although the anthropomorphization of gods had long been accomplished, in hieroglyphs the names of deities continued to be written by means of pictures of animals and cult objects throughout Egyptian history.

A complete abandonment of the old zoomorphic conception of gods seemed difficult to the Egyptians. They could hardly ever discard an old idea in favour of a new one; they either allowed both to exist side by side, disregarding a logical contradiction often implied by their mere co-existence, or, whenever possible, they combined the two ideas in a composite whole. Thus the anthropomorphized gods were given a human body, but only seldom a human head, this being mostly replaced by that of the animal in whose form the god originally used to appear: the human body of Horus bears the head of a falcon, that of Anubis a dog's head and Khnum appears with the head of a ram. The addition of the animal head to the body was cleverly executed, the actual join being concealed by the folds of the headdress and its lappets.

The goddess Hathor received a human head, but this was provided with the two horns of a cow and the sun disk between them. The goddess Mafdet was entirely human, but clad in the skin of her cat-like animal, and Hat-mehit was human too, but carried her creature, a fish, on her head. This solution was adopted for anthropomorphic deities which formerly appeared as inanimate objects. They became entirely human in form, but carried their particular fetish on their heads: in the case of Neith it was a shield with two arrows crossed over it, while the head of the goddess Seshat was surmounted by a star-shaped object fixed on the top of a pole.

Finally, certain gods never appear except in human form with a human head, like Min of Koptos, Ptah of Memphis, Atum of Heliopolis, Amun of Thebes. We must assume that these gods were represented as entirely human from the very beginning. In view of the course of development which the ideas concerning gods seem to have followed in Egypt it is difficult to escape the conclusion that these gods belong to a relatively late stage in the evolution of the Egyptian religion, though to one which still precedes the beginning of history. It is, however, only in the case of Min and Ptah that actual pictorial evidence of their great antiquity is available. We have seen that statues and pictures of Min in human form date from the Ist Dynasty or earlier, and the earliest known representation of Ptah is found on an alabaster bowl from Tarkhan dating from about the reign of Udymu, the fifth king of the Ist Dynasty. Atum is attested in the Old Kingdom, but Amun only appears in the Middle Kingdom.

The difference of date between Min and Ptah on one hand and Atum and Amun on the other is further confirmed by the way in which the problem of their representation in human form is solved. For while Atum, Amun and the gods who, though anthropomorphized, still retain the heads of their animals, are represented walking with legs and hands well articulated (in short as living beings), Min and Ptah always appear as statues on pedestals, with legs joined together and hands hardly protruding from the body. This traditional representation of Min and Ptah, therefore, goes back to a primitive period, when the sculptor's technique was not sufficiently advanced to enable the limbs to be separated from the body of the statue. Among the other gods only Osiris, and even he not consistently, shares this peculiarity with Min and Ptah, and this fact seems the best proof of his early origin. He appears in written documents only in the second half of the Vth Dynasty; the occurrence of a *djed*-pillar in a tomb of the Ist Dynasty at Helwan, which has been quoted as a proof of the early origin of Osiris, is not sufficient, since the *djed*-pillar becomes associated with Osiris only at a much later date.

The destinies of individual gods in historical times, the nearly complete disappearance of some, the rise into prominence of others and to some extent also the gradual change in the nature of some of them, were largely caused or influenced by the political development and changes in the country. These led first to the unification of separate localities into nomes, which subsequently merged into two divisions, namely Upper and Lower Egypt, and finally became united into a single kingdom at the beginning of the historical period. These political changes brought the local gods into closer contact. The gods of the capitals of the nomes became the heads of all the other gods in the nomes, and the god of the capital of the united country became its chief god. While in the course of this development some gods—as has already been pointed out—were overshadowed by more important ones or were absorbed by them and fell into oblivion, priests and worshippers of other gods strove to preserve their local deities from a similar fate. They declared their god to be merely another form or aspect of an important deity and differing from him in no essential respect—an attitude adopted especially in cases where the two rival gods displayed from the very outset some features in common. Various degrees of identification, assimilation and fusion resulted in this way. Thus a number of lion-goddesses became identified with the cow-goddess Hathor. The name of the god assimilated or absorbed either disappeared altogether or became a mere epithet of the god into whom he was assimilated; in this way Ptah, the god of Memphis, absorbed Sokar, the necropolis god of a neighbouring locality, and thenceforward often appeared as Ptah-Sokar.

Another favourite means of preserving an old god or goddess was to bring them into family relationship with the powerful god, and so to create couples or triads in which a god and goddess played the part of husband and wife, while a third deity was sometimes added to them as their son; *e.g.*, at Antinoupolis the frog-goddess Heket became the wife of the ram-god Khnum and at Memphis Ptah obtained the lion-goddess Sakhmet as wife and the god Nefertem became their son.

The union of Egypt was achieved by a king of Hierakonpolis,

whose falcon-god, Horus, was a sky-god. Horus manifested himself in the person of the Upper Egyptian king who besides his personal name bore a Horus-name in his quality of an incarnation of Horus. Horus, the god of the conqueror, became the state deity of the united country. The union, however, must have been accomplished not without the essential help of the towns and nomes of Ombos and Khmun (Hermopolis), because their gods, Sētekh and Thoth respectively, were entitled to claim some importance even in the united kingdom. Such an importance was never denied to Thoth, who always remained one of the high deities. Sētekh, on the other hand, claimed the title of the "Lord of Upper Egypt" and became a rival of Horus to such a degree that the king also became his manifestation and was, from the time of the Ist Dynasty, a united personification of Horus-Sētekh.

With King Khasekhemui of the IInd Dynasty the usual Horus-name becomes a Horus-Sētekh name and the King bears it even in an inscription on a granite door jamb in the temple of Horus at Hieraconpolis. At one point Sētekh even gained a predominance over Horus; this is reflected by the fact that the King Peribsen of the IInd Dynasty replaced the Horus-name by a Sētekh name. A return to the Horus-name by later kings shows that this predominance on the part of Sētekh was only temporary, but the rivalry of Horus and Sētekh must have been the cause of the later introduction of Sētekh into the myth of Osiris and Horus as their enemy and rival.

Egyptologists are still unable to agree on the most remote origin of Horus. While some hold him to be one of the numerous falcon-gods whose cult existed in the predynastic period at various places in Upper and Lower Egypt alike, and declare Horus to be of Upper Egyptian origin, others interpret the evidence as pointing towards the existence at a time in prehistory of a Lower Egyptian kingdom with Pe (later called Buto) as its capital and with Horus as its chief god. This Lower Egyptian kingdom conquered Upper Egypt of which the capital Enboyet (later Ombos) was the original seat of the cult of Setekh, and transplanted the cult of Horus from Lower Egypt to Edfu (or Behdet) in the upper country. According to this theory, therefore, Horus was originally the Lower Egyptian national god, and of Lower Egyptian origin, and when Egypt subsequently separated into two kingdoms, both parts worshipped Horus as their chief god. Horus of Behdet (called "the Behdetite") played an extremely important part in the kingship and religion of the dynastic period, but he began to do so only from the time of the IIIrd Dynasty and no trace of him occurs in the Pyramid texts, the very extensive collection of religious literature preserved from the Vth Dynasty. It is, therefore, perhaps better to admit that we have as yet no certain knowledge of how and when the cult of Horus came to Behdet and to wait for new material to decide between the two conflicting theories.

Menes, however, after the final union of Egypt, moved to Memphis, which for a number of centuries remained the capital and even later was always counted among the largest and most important towns in the country. It was, therefore, not difficult for the chief god of the town, Ptah, to establish his position firmly in the new state and to maintain it throughout Egyptian history while keeping his individual character unaltered and uncontaminated by that of any other Egyptian god.

Another important religious centre, the town of Yonew (Heliopolis), lay not far from Memphis. Here the sun-god Rē was worshipped. He was conceived not in animal or human form, but as the celestial body itself and, when necessary, was represented as the solar disk. This cult seems to have attained great popularity in Lower Egypt even before the Ist Dynasty and to have influenced the conception of the Lower Egyptian kingship. When the capital was established at Memphis the victorious Upper Egyptian kings, who personified the sky-god Horus, came under the influence of the Heliopolitan sun-cult. An outcome of this political development was the creation of a god named Harakhte, "Horus of the Horizon", who was identified with Rē, a composite god Rē-Harakhte resulting from this fusion. The king, who had previously been identified with Horus (not Harakhte) was now declared to be the son of Rē.

It is impossible to decide at what moment solar conceptions pervaded the idea of kingship. The earliest evidence for such a tendency seems to be the Horus-name of the second king of the IInd Dynasty, Rē-neb (perhaps to be translated "Rē is Lord"), Djoser of the IIIrd Dynasty bears as a title "the golden

C

Rē". Both Rē-neb and Djoser, therefore, appear to have identified themselves with Rē rather than to have considered themselves as descendants of the sun-god. The identification, however, was not of long duration, for it was completely abandoned
by subsequent kings. The first kings officially called "son of
Rē" are Khafrē and Menkaurē of the IVth Dynasty; the epithet
is further borne by three kings towards the end of the Vth
Dynasty (Neuserrē, Djedkerē and Unis). From the VIth
Dynasty onwards the title "son of Rē" is borne by all kings
and becomes finally an integral part of the royal titulary. It
introduces the king's birth-name and thus clearly shows that
the king was born as a son of Rē. But as early as Djedefrē of
the IVth Dynasty many kings had names compounded with Rē,
sometimes as their birth-names, or when these did not include
Rē, they adopted the name on ascending the throne. According to a late tale the kings of the Vth Dynasty were sons of the
god Rē and the wife of a priest of Rē. The tale thus reflects
the victory of the Rē-cult under this dynasty, most of whose
kings built sanctuaries to the god after the model of the Rē-
temple of Heliopolis. Though this dominant position of Rē
weakened towards the end of the Dynasty, the sun-cult had
already permeated the whole Egyptian religion and led to
identification of many local gods with Rē.

While in the earlier representations "the Behdetite" is still
a distinct falcon-god hovering over the head of the king, in
later scenes this attribute is applied to the winged solar disk,
whose two wings symbolically protect Upper and Lower Egypt.
The winged disk clearly represents the actual person of the
king as immanent in the visible sun; it bears the epithet "great
god", like the king, and is intimately connected with the king's
name. All this indicates a complete fusion of Rē, Horus and the
king.

At about the same time as it found a means of reconciliation
with the conception of the king as the god Horus, the solar
religion of Heliopolis succeeded in reaching a compromise with
a new cult, in fact a new religion which was irresistibly spreading from the centre of the Delta towards the south, the religion
of Osiris. Osiris came from Djedu, the capital of the IXth
nome of Lower Egypt; "Lord of Djedu" is his old title and the

town was later called Per-Usire (the Greek form of this being Busiris), "House of Osiris". Nevertheless, Djedu was probably not his original home, since the proper god of Djedu was Andjeti, who is represented in human form as a ruler with his insignia, a long crooked sceptre in one hand and a whip in the other, with two feathers on his head. Andjeti was, however, very early absorbed by Osiris and his name became a mere epithet of that god.

A circumstance that favoured the absorption was that Osiris too was entirely human in form. He also is shown with the Upper Egyptian white crown to which two feathers are attached on both sides and which is set on a pair of ram's horns. But there is an important difference between Andjeti and Osiris: while the former represents a living ruler, Osiris is always shown as a dead person, standing, wrapped in a long white royal cloak, the two arms holding the sceptre. His name Usire, of which Osiris is the Greek form, seems to mean "Seat of the Eye"; it has the appearance of a human name and it is probable that Osiris was originally a human king who became deified after his death. A myth was woven round his person which is less concerned with his former life and rule as a king of Egypt than with his death and subsequent resurrection after which he became a ruler in the realm of the dead. No systematic exposition of this myth is known from Egyptian sources, our chief authority in this respect being Plutarch in his "On Isis and Osiris"; frequent allusions, however, occur in Egyptian texts of all periods which show that Plutarch's account agrees essentially with the Egyptian belief.

The wife of Osiris was his sister Isis (Egn. Eset) whose name means "Seat"; she appears, therefore, to be merely a personification of Osiris' royal throne. His other sister Nephthys (Egn. Nebthut, "Lady of the Castle") was probably only an artificial creation and a counterpart to her husband Sētekh, Osiris' brother, who with his confederates killed Osiris, but was defeated by Osiris' son, Horus, after a long fight; Horus thus avenged his father and succeeded him on the throne of Egypt.

There were two versions of the death of Osiris: according to one he was killed at Nedit, the situation of which is unknown, and his corpse was cut in pieces and thrown into the Nile; according to the other he was drowned in the river. In both cases his resurrection was effected by magic. The connection with the Nile was the result of an early interpretation of Osiris as a god of the Nile and its inundation, as well as of the vegetation which regularly follows the Nile flood. This character of Osiris as a nature god is apparent from his earliest appearance in Egyptian texts at the end of the Vth Dynasty. But the kingly character is the most striking and constant feature, and every king after his death was identified with Osiris and, like Osiris, was imagined to rise again in the next Life.

In the social revolution following the end of the Old Kingdom this conception of the identity of the dead king with Osiris was extended first to other members of the royal family and to the aristocracy and later to commoners, so that by the Middle Kingdom every Egyptian, male and female alike, became Osiris after death and was called "Osiris so and so". After the penetration of the cult of Osiris into Upper Egypt its most important centre became Abydos, where Osiris gradually superseded the old funerary god Khenti-Amentiu. Various places mentioned in the myth of Osiris were identified with actual places in the vicinity of Abydos and one of the early royal tombs, that of King Djer of the Ist Dynasty, was considered to be the tomb of Osiris, although a number of other towns in Egypt also claimed to have tombs in which individual parts of his dismembered body were buried. On the other hand the mere fact that the tombs of the kings of the Ist and IInd Dynasties were situated at Abydos does not prove that these kings identified themselves or were identified with Osiris or that the cult of Osiris existed in Abydos in their time.

Since the character of Osiris as a local god, if indeed it ever existed, had completely disappeared, no Egyptian, whoever his actual town-god might be, would find any difficulty in embracing the Osirian belief. Nor was Osiris ever a rival to any other god, with the consequence that his cult could spread unchecked concurrently with a belief in other gods. A clear distinction was drawn between Osiris and the remainder of the pantheon: Osiris was a dead king and god, and as such was concerned only with the dead and with dominion and justice in the netherworld; his son, Horus, incarnated in the reigning king, was concerned with the living and so were the other gods with whom the king was identified.

When the nomarchs of En-mont (now Armant), south of Thebes, again unified Egypt after a long period of anarchy and founded the XIth Dynasty, the god of their native town Mont came into prominence and his cult spread from En-Mont to the three neighbouring towns, Thebes, Medamud and Tod. This re-unification was achieved by force of arms and from that time Mont came to be regarded as a god of war. The XIth Dynasty was, however, ousted from power by an official of Theban origin, Amenemhet by name, and he and his successors favoured another, hitherto obscure, god of Thebes, namely Amun. His history in Thebes can be traced back to the reign of Intef I of the XIth Dynasty, when his name is first found on the grave stela of that king. He had, however, been introduced into Thebes from Hermopolis (Khmun), where he and his female counterpart, Amaunet, were members of an ogdoad comprising four male and four female deities who personified the prim-ordial ocean and its qualities (darkness, endlessness and mysteri-ous invisibility). The reason for this transplantation of Amun to a new locality was to give the newly united country a supreme god shared by all inhabitants in common. Amun was made "chief of the gods" and to his Hermopolitan character were added features taken from other important gods of the coun-try: the Memphite Ptah, himself already identified with the primordial god Tatjenen, the Heliopolitan Rē and Min of Koptos.

During the reigns of Amenemhet I and his successors Amun would have quickly attained the dominant position intended for him by the unifier of the country if the kings of the dynasty had not moved their capital far to the north to the entrance of the Fayyum, which they opened for cultivation. By so doing they fostered the importance of the local Fayyum god Subek and of the gods of Memphis and Heliopolis against Amun, although he had become "lord of the thrones of the two lands".

The real ascendancy of Amun began with the victory of the Theban XVIIIth Dynasty over the Hyksos and the Egyptian conquest in Asia. The rivalry of Rē was at that time eliminated by the association of Amun with Rē as Amon-Rē. It was in his name and with his help that the kings of the dynasty founded the Empire of which Amonrē became the supreme god and the "king of the gods". Two great temples were built for him at Karnak (Egn. Opet-isut) and Luxor (Egn. Opet-rīset, "southern Opet") and magnificently endowed from the tribute of Asia. His position was thus ensured until the end of Egypt as an independent nation.

CHAPTER II

CHARACTER OF THE GODS

In the preceding chapter we have seen a host of Egyptian gods emerging gradually from the darkness of the prehistoric period as written records begin to flow in. They are all distinguished from each other by their names, festivals and the localities to which their worship was originally, and in many cases throughout the whole history of the country, attached. Apart from these external features it is rather difficult to determine their individual nature. The sources of the Old Kingdom are silent about this, so that it must be reconstructed from documents of a much later date, though as early as the end of the Vth Dynasty some valuable information is supplied by the Pyramid texts.

It is impossible to sketch a picture of a belief which is uniform and logical in all its details, and valid for the whole of Egypt, for such a uniform belief never existed. The Egyptian religion is not the creation of a single thinker, but an outcome of local political and cultural divergences and there was never a strong enough force in Egypt to eliminate all local beliefs or to unite them in a general theological system equally binding to Egyptians of all classes and all places. Owing to the temporary political, economic and cultural power of their town some of the religious systems ended by being accepted outside the boundaries of their place of origin, but this does not imply that the local beliefs of the territory into which they spread were given up. On the contrary, the new system was nearly always superimposed upon the old in such a way that the god or gods of the old system were identified with those of the new.

"Identified" is possibly not quite the right expression, it is perhaps more accurate to say that by degrees the old god came to be looked upon as merely another form of the new one, or as a part or another aspect of him, or as being contained in him. That these ideas could only be vague and ill-defined is evident: they are above human understanding and the Egyptians, with their general lack of definition and precise logical thinking, could not be expected to feel an urgent need for a clear sequence of events and definition in these matters.

It would be unfair to the Egyptians to conclude from the large number of their deities which first appear in the form of animals or inanimate objects that they considered these very animals or objects as gods. Such beliefs were imputed to them by other peoples of the ancient world, notably by the Greeks, and for such beliefs they were later ridiculed, despised and persecuted by Christians. It is obvious that no mind, however primitive, can consider objects, animals or even human beings as more than a visible manifestation or seat of an abstract divine force. The Egyptians, like other human beings, sought to get into contact with this supernatural force and saw that the best way to achieve this was by choosing some concrete and easily visualized rallying-point round which the attributes of personality could be grouped, to use Sir Alan Gardiner's words. It must, of course, be admitted that the illiterate and primitive Egyptian peasants may at all times have taken these personifications of divinity more literally than they were intended to. The conceptions held by the common people always tend to give material form to the more abstract ideas of those thinking and learned individuals who constitute the class which gives a more definite shape to rather vague religious feeling. Also for the purposes of art—and art was an important factor in Egypt—some material personification of deities was indispensable, and if the human bodies of gods kept the heads of various animals, this was certainly largely because it was a convenient means of distinguishing their various personalities. That the head of the animal should in some way recall the qualities attributed to the god is only natural.

Egyptian gods had their origin in the country, and though it has sometimes been suggested that some of them came from abroad, it has never been possible to demonstrate the foreign origin of any of them. Their names are Egyptian and can be explained from the Egyptian language. They are, therefore, purely national and such they remained till the expansion of the Egyptian political power introduced their cult into neighbouring countries, namely Nubia and the Sudan, Palestine and

Syria. But in the original isolation of the country they were concerned only with Egypt and the Egyptians, for by the "*earth*" over which they ruled and the "*men*" with whom they were in relation, Egypt and the Egyptians themselves were meant. And just as no records have reached us of the worship of a god having been spread by force within the country itself, so we never hear of Egyptians preaching their own religion to other peoples as the only true faith. Such an attitude was entirely foreign to the Egyptian mind. Of course, individual Egyptian gods were believed to help the king to win victories and make conquests in foreign countries and to foster his own and his country's political power, but not Egyptian religious beliefs.

Egyptians were tolerant to each other within Egypt itself and they were equally tolerant to the gods of a conquered country. Naturally, Egyptian settlers and garrisons abroad built sanctuaries there to their own gods, but towards the native gods they behaved as they so often did in Egypt towards the god or goddess of another town: they simply considered them as different names and forms of their own Egyptian deities. It is clear that in these circumstances no heresy could arise, and with the exception of a short period under and immediately after Ekhnaton, nothing is known of religious persecution of any kind in Egypt. It is not clear whether Ekhnaton's religion was intended to be a universal religion destined for all the peoples of the Egyptian empire, though certain features suggest this, and it is curious that forcible measures were adopted both for its dissemination in Egypt and for its suppression later.

Surrounded by nature on which his existence depended, an Egyptian saw divine forces all round him inhabiting the cosmic elements and phenomena, above all the earth, sky and air, the Nile floods and the sun and moon. These, personified in human form, gave origin to a number of cosmic deities of such general importance that they were not attached to any definite locality, and being present everywhere had no need of an organized form of worship or a temple at all.

In the poetic phantasy of an oriental people they behaved like human beings and it is as human beings that they were spoken of. Myths arose around their personalities and deeds, and the Egyptians did not even shrink from imputing to them the human shortcomings and weaknesses to which they were subject themselves. Only a few relatively late myths of this kind have come down to us complete, but innumerable allusions to mythical events in texts show that myths were already flourishing at the end of the Vth Dynasty.

Egyptian gods and the world which they animated were not considered to be eternal as far as past eternity was concerned. They existed in the present and certain natural phenomena occurred with regularity; such repetition could also be safely assumed for a long period back into the past. But Egyptian logic required that there must once have been a moment when the element in question originated, when a phenomenon of nature took place for the first time; that was its *"first occurrence"*, in other words the creation of the visible world. Before that there must have been a time when there were no sky or earth, no gods or men, no air, no overflowing of the Nile, not even the *"name of a thing"*, and consequently not a thing itself.

The way in which things, gods and men had originated interested the Egyptians very much. Opinions about this were divided, and theologians in various religious centres evolved theories and myths to explain the creation of the world. The most important cosmogonies were three in number, those of Hermopolis, Heliopolis and Memphis.

According to the Hermopolitan belief, there was nothing at the beginning except chaos, which was imagined either as a person or as an element. It consisted of primordial water, Nun, who was, therefore, called the *Old one who took origin first.* This chaos was characterized by an immense depth, endlessness, darkness and invisibility, each of them personified by a pair of primordial deities—male and female—called respectively by the names of the four characteristics in question: Nun and Naunet, Huh and Hauhet, Kuk and Kakwet, Amun and Amaunet. It was after these primordial gods that the town, named in Greek times Hermopolis, took its Egyptian name of Khmun, that is, the town of Eight. We do not know the continuation of the cosmogony of Hermopolis, the reason being that very early, during the First Intermediate Period, it was mingled with the cosmogony of Heliopolis, which supplied the rest of creation from its own system.

Atum, the god of Heliopolis, emerged from chaos as or on a hill. He mated with his hand and spat out the god Show and the goddess Tfenet, and from these two further gods descended by natural birth. Atum, whóse name perhaps signifies "*the Accomplished One*", was absolute. To him belonged three important features: he was the *oldest*, the *only one*, and came into existence *by himself*. All other gods were younger, he, therefore, ruled over them and was "*Lord of All*". According to current opinion, Show was the air and Tfenet the moisture, and with them began the orderly world. As air, Show was the life-giving and life-creating power, for all life depended on him. His palpable manifestation (or *bai*) was the wind and the breath, he was endless and invisible. Show separated the sky from the earth by lifting up the sky and filling up the whole space between them.

It was difficult to decide who was the oldest, the chaos Nun, Atum or Show and the only remedy seemed to be to accept that Atum was all the time immanent in Nun, and that Show was born at the same time as Atum and was, therefore, as old as he. With Show and Tfenet, Atum becomes three, all being of one substance, a transcendental conception which reminds one very much of the controversy among Christians of the fourth and fifth centuries concerning the relation and precedence of the three Persons of the Trinity. Egyptian theology finally discarded the unnatural creation of Show and maintained that he had been breathed out, which seemed more consistent with his nature as god of the air, and that Atum made him by his magic power.

Since the Heliopolitan theology had already declared Atum to be only another aspect of the sun-god Rē, the two resulting in a composite god Rē-Atum, his emergence from Nun meant nothing else than the appearance of light, which dispelled the darkness of the chaotic waters.

The personified universe is, therefore, represented by the Egyptians as Show holding above him on his uplifted arms his daughter Nut, the goddess of the sky, while his son Geb, the god of the earth, lies at his feet.

In Hermopolitan theology, Hermopolis itself was the place where the primordial hill first appeared and thus the first step towards the creation of the universe was made. It formed there a sacred district, rectangular and surrounded by a high wall within which was the replica of the scene of creation: a lake called "*Lake of the Two Knives*" representing Nun, and in it the "*Island of Flames*" with a hill, the name of the island clearly pointing to the fact that light originated there. The idea of primordial water and the emergence of a hill from it had been suggested by the yearly overflowing of the waters of the Nile, at the end of which the land gradually appeared.

There were several such primordial hills in Egypt. In Heliopolis its image in historic times was a "*sand-hill*" with a stone of conical shape, the prototype of the later obelisk, on the top of which Atum appeared first when he emerged from Nun, according to one tale in the form of a mythical bird, the Phoenix. In Memphis it was the whole Memphitic district, personified as the god Tatjenen, "*the land rising* (i.e. from the primordial water)", and when Thebes became the capital, it also had a primordial hill which was situated within the temple district of Medinet Habu on the west bank of the Nile.

Sometime between the IIIrd and Vth Dynasties, when Memphis was the capital, an imperative need was felt to attempt a conciliation between the Heliopolitan theogony, in which Atum was the creator, and the Memphite theology with Ptah at the head, so that Ptah should become the creator. Eight of the gods of creation from Nun down to Nefertem and including Atum, were declared to be contained in Ptah; *they have their forms in Ptah*, are nothing but Ptah. Atum in particular is the heart and tongue of Ptah, the divine forms of the two being the gods Horus and Thoth respectively. "*Creation took place through the heart and the tongue as an image of Atum. But the greatest is Ptah who supplied all gods and their faculties* (kas) *with [life] through this heart and this tongue—the heart and tongue through which Horus and Thoth took origin as Ptah. His Ennead* (of gods) *is in front of him as teeth and lips which are nothing else but the seed and hands of Atum, for the Ennead of Atum was born of his seed and his fingers, but the Ennead are the teeth and the lips in his mouth which has pronounced the names of all things, from which Show and Tfenet have come forth and which has fashioned the Ennead."*

"In this way were fashioned all gods and his Ennead was completed. For every divine word sprang from what the heart had pondered over and the tongue had ordained. And in this way the faculties (kas) *were made and their female counterparts* (hemset) *were determined, which make all food and all supply through this word, and in this way also that man was declared just who does what is liked, and that man wrong who does what is hated. So also is life given to the peaceable and death to the wrongdoer. Thus it has been found and recognized that his (Ptah's) form is greater than that of (other) gods. And thus was Ptah satisfied after he had made all things and all divine words."*

Interspersed in this account of creation by Ptah are sections of the following justification which in its whole gives evidence of a surprisingly accurate knowledge of physiological phenomena:

"For it is so that the heart and tongue have power over all members, considering that (the heart) is in every body and (the tongue) in every mouth, of all gods, all men, all cattle, all worms and (all) living beings, while (the heart) conceives thoughts and (the tongue) commands freely. The seeing of the eyes, the hearing of the ears and the breathing of the nose report to the heart. And it is the heart which produces all cognition and it is the tongue which repeats that which has been thought out by the heart. And (in this way) is produced any work and any craft, the activity of the arms, the walking of the feet, the movement of all members according to the order which has been thought out by the heart, has come forth through the tongue and put into effect with a view of (accomplishing) all things."

The creation of the world by Ptah is presented in a highly intellectual manner as a combined action of conceiving through the intelligence (the seat of which is the heart) and creating through the spoken word or command (the seat of which is the tongue). Other gods are only this heart and tongue, lips and teeth of Ptah.

Two thousand years after its composition this theological treatise was still considered so important that at the order of the Ethiopian king Shabaka it was transferred from a damaged papyrus manuscript to a hard black stone slab. Indeed, it certainly has no parallel at such an early stage in the history of mankind.

In the minds of Egyptians the *"time of the gods"* or the *"time of the god"* had really existed. Not only is it often referred to when they speak of something that happened long ago, but the time of particular gods is named: Atum, Geb, Osiris, Horus and most often Rē. Nor do they always mean a vague reference to time immemorial. It was evidently believed that the gods had lived on earth and actually ruled over it, or more precisely over Egypt; indeed both the priest Manethos of Sebennytus, who in Ptolemaic times wrote a history of Egypt in the Greek language, and the fragmentary papyrus from about the reign of Ramesses II, now preserved at the Turin Museum, prefix to their lists of the reigns of human kings a list of gods with numbers of years, in the papyrus those of their length of life, in Manethos those of their reign. In the Turin papyrus ten gods were originally listed, but the names of seven only have survived: Geb, Osiris, Sētekh, Horus, Thoth, the goddess Ma'et and another Horus; the extracts made from Manethos, however, make it probable that Ptah, Rē and Show headed the list. It is interesting that while Thoth was supposed to have lived for 3,726 years, Geb only lived for 1,773 and Horus for 300.

Myths were also current which related events from the reigns of various gods, especially that of Rē, the two best and most complete being the myth of the winged sun-disk and the myth of the destruction of mankind.

The myth of the winged sun-disk, contained in a long hieroglyphic inscription on the wall of the temple of Edfu, dates in its present form from the reign of Ptolemy XVI Caesarion, but undoubtedly consists of various much earlier elements. Like a historical inscription it starts with a date, year 363 of the king of Upper and Lower Egypt, Rē-Harakhte. This is the usual name of the sun-god, but in the inscription no reference is made to the sun. Rē-Harakhte is spoken of as an entirely earthly king. Rē-Harakhte was in Nubia with his army when he was informed of a plot against him in Egypt. Who the plotters were is nowhere expressly stated, but it appears that the author imagines them as some kind of demons or inferior deities. Rē-Harakhte sailed downstream in his boat

and landed near Edfu. His son, Horus, was with him and Rē-
Harakhte charged him to fight the enemy. Horus flew to the
sky in the form of a winged sun-disk and descrying the enemy
from there, he threw himself down on them so fiercely that they
could not resist his attack and fled. Horus returned to the boat
of his father and at the suggestion of the god Thoth was
granted the name of Horus Behdety, that is, Horus of Edfu.
Rē-Harakhte inspected the slain enemies in the company of
the goddess Astarte, but the fight was far from being ended,
for the surviving enemies entered the water and changed into
crocodiles and hippopotami. They attacked the boat of Rē-
Harakhte, but were slaughtered by Horus and his followers
armed with harpoons on ropes. Horus then assumed the form
of the winged disk at the prow of the boat flanked by the two
uraeus-goddesses, Nekhbet and Wedjoyet, and pursued the
enemies through Upper and Lower Egypt defeating them at
various places, at Thebes, Denderah, Hebenu (in the XVIth
Upper Egyptian nome) and at Meret (in the XIXth nome).

Here suddenly Horus, son of Osiris and Isis, appears at
the side of Horus of Behdet (Edfu) and the chief of the enemies
is Sētekh. Sētekh changed into a serpent and disappeared into
the ground and the fighting went on through the XXth nome
towards Thel, a town on the frontier of Asia, and as far as the
sea. After having been victorious in Lower Egypt, Horus and
his followers sailed upstream to Nubia to repress a rebellion
there and having succeeded in this, Rē-Harakhte and his
followers landed again at Edfu, where Rē-Harakhte decided
that as a reward for the eminent services which Horus had
rendered in defeating the enemy the winged disk should in
future be placed on all temples and shrines of gods and goddesses
in Upper and Lower Egypt to keep enemies away from them.

The whole is an aetiological narrative to explain the origin
of the winged disk, the form under which Horus of Behdet
appeared, especially above the doors of all late temples. Throughout the fighting, there is no question of men, all the persons
taking part are gods or demons. Nevertheless, it has been suggested that the events related in the myth had a basis in historical events, which indeed seems possible; but opinions are
divided as to the date to which they should be assigned, some

scholars favouring the clash between the worship of Horus and that of Sētekh under King Peribsen of the IInd Dynasty, others proposing the Egyptian revolt against the Persian occupation a few decades before Alexander the Great.

While in the myth of Horus the Behdetite a human enemy has possibly been transferred to the realm of spirits and demons, the myth of the destruction of mankind by Rē expressly refers to a misdemeanour of human beings towards the supreme god. It was at the time when *"men and gods were one thing"*, that is, when they mixed together on earth. Rē had grown old and men began to conspire against him. But Rē knew their thoughts and called the gods together to ask their advice as to what he should do with men. The gods suggested that he should send his eye, that is the sun, as the goddess Hathor, to smite the conspirators. The goddess was sent against men, showed her power over them (whence she obtained the name Sakhmet, *"the Powerful One"*), and came back, intending to go again and eradicate mankind completely. At this moment Rē took pity on men and sent fast messengers to Elephantine to bring a great quantity of red fruits called *didi*. He ordered 7,000 jugs of beer to be made and the fruit to be put into the beer so that it looked like blood. Early on the morning of the day when the goddess was about to go to destroy men, he caused the intoxicating liquid to be poured over the fields, and when the goddess came she drank of it and became drunk. She could not see her victims and mankind was saved.

Rē, however, still indignant with men, retired to heaven, which the myth represents as a cow. Rē sat on the back of this heavenly animal leaving the god Thoth on earth as his representative. And Thoth brought light again to the people in darkness, appearing to them as the moon. It can easily be seen that the whole story is a mythological explanation of the disappearance of the sun at sunset and its replacement by the moonlight at night.

The existence of men side by side with the gods at the time of their sojourn on earth is assumed everywhere, but so far no detailed account of the creation of man is known. Men were of course created by the gods as everything else was, sometimes they are even called *"cattle of the god"* or *"cattle of Rē"*. The latter designation brings them into close relation with Rē, so that their creation by Rē must have been generally assumed. In fact, in the myth of the Destruction of Mankind, the origin of men (in Egyptian, *röme*) is explained by a pun on the tears (*rïme*) of the sun-god, and elsewhere it is said of men that they *"have come forth from his eye"*, while animals and things were only *"made"* by him. But older than this role of Rē is the belief that the ram-god Khnum formed men on the potter's wheel and that in this way he still fashioned every child to be born. This is only a refinement of the original ascription to Khnum of the creation of all living things, on account of the extraordinary engendering power of his sacred animal, the ram.

Men, therefore, were created by the gods and even contained something of the divine substance. It was not impossible for them to become gods themselves, not of course during their lifetime—among the living only the king was a god—but after their death. We know of several such cases, in each case it is a man of some high rank, usually a vizier, the highest official and representative of the king in the country. An example is the worship of Kagemni at the end of the Old Kingdom, when devotees, whose names in many cases were formed by means of Gemen, a shortening of Kagemni, and who were perhaps all members of his family, had their tombs placed all round his mastaba near Memphis. He is, however, not called *"god"*, but was perhaps something like a saint.

The worship of another vizier of about the same time, Isi, was still flourishing centuries after his time in the town of Edfu where he had probably spent the end of his life and where he was buried. A large number of devotees set up their stelae or chapels in his tomb and addressed their prayers to him as well as to Horus of Edfu and Osiris, calling him *"Isi, the living god"*. There is no proof that his worship survived the Second Intermediate Period. Imhotep, the vizier and architect of King Djoser of the IIIrd Dynasty, and Amenhotep, Hapu's son, the vizier of King Amenhotep III of the XVIIIth, were deified as late as the Saite Period, but their cult was still very popular in Ptolemaic Egypt, and even among the Greeks, who called them Imuthes and Amenothes Paapios (*i.e.*, son of Hapu) respectively. They represented the wisdom of the ances-

D

tors. Imhotep became a god of medicine and was identified with the Greek Asklepios, but as early as the New Kingdom he is found as a patron of scribes, who used to offer a libation to him before starting to write, and he was believed to have been the son of the god Ptah himself and a lady, Khreduonkh.

For the Egyptians the primaeval water Nun still existed. Together with the sea ("*the Great Green*") it surrounded the earth which floated on Nun in the form of a flat disk. Nun, therefore, also stretched under the earth and was found as water when digging to a certain depth below the surface. And the Nile, and especially its flood waters, which inundated the land of Egypt every year, were nothing else than Nun. According to a very early belief which theology never completely abandoned, the water of the Nile sprang from two sources in the region of the First Cataract near the town of Elephantine.

The earth was bounded all round by a chain of high mountains on which rested the sky (*pet*, also *hrēyet* "*the upper* (*i.e.*, sky)") often personified as the goddess Nut. There was another, corresponding sky beneath the earth (Egn. *Naunet*). The world under the earth was called *Dēt* (formerly read *Duat*). The sun or the sun-god appeared in the morning in the east between two mountains and started its journey across the sky in a barque called *mandjet*. The sun is usually represented as a red (*i.e.*, burning) disk, the sun-god sometimes inside the disk, either entirely in human form or with a ram's head, sometimes as a disk between the forelegs of a beetle, the scarab. The scarab (the modern scientific name of which is *Ateuchus Sacer*) was a favourite form for the sun-god. His name, *Kheperer* was derived from the verb *khoper* "to come into existence" and thus appropriately expressed the notion of the sun-god, who first came into existence independently at the beginning of the world and has done so again every morning ever since; moreover, the actual beetle can often be seen pushing before him a ball of dung in which he hides his eggs, the seed of a new life, and which strongly recalls the sun-disk.

Various gods accompany the sun-god in his boat and act as its crew. Usually they are Geb, Thoth and personifications of the faculties of the sun-god, especially those of his magic power (*Hīke*), of cognisance (*Sia*) and of his authoritative and creative

utterance (*Hu*). Reaching the western horizon, the sun-god
passes from the day-barque into the night-barque (called
meseket), or is seen as a disk handed over from one boat by the
personified goddess of the east into the arms of the goddess of
the west standing in the night-boat. The sun-god then pursues
his journey under the earth in the night-boat, illuminating the
darkness of Dēt, to appear in the east again at the beginning of
the next day.

Other very popular ideas were that the sun was a child
who entered the mouth of the sky-goddess, Nut, in the evening,
passed during the night through her body and was born from
her lap again in the morning, or a young calf of the sky-goddess
when she is imagined as a heavenly cow.

There was a considerable intermingling of these different
conceptions, and it is, therefore, not surprising to see the story
referred to above of the destruction of mankind accompanied
by an illustration in which the anthropomorphic sun-god
travels in his day-boat on the belly of the heavenly cow.

The idea interpreting the sunset as the swallowing-up of
the sun by the sky-goddess also underlies a more crude explanation of the movement of the stars. They are little pigs who
disappear into the mouth of a heavenly sow (the goddess Nut);
she eats them up in the morning and bears them again before
the night begins. That is why the Egyptian word for "evening"
(*mesut*) means literally "the time of the birth".

But the stars too were divine beings. They were divided into
two groups. One group were called "*those who can never set*";
they were the circumpolar stars which in fact never disappear
or can disappear from the sky. The other group, "*those who
can never become weary*" were the stars which rise at various
times in the east, are visible for a part of the night and then set
again in the west. The two groups form respectively the crews
which attend the sun-boat during its day and night journeys.
"Those who can never set" accompany the god during his day
crossing, when they are invisible, being obliterated by the glow
of the sun; "those who can never become weary" belong to
the crew of the night-boat, they disappear one after another in
the west to join the barque during its journey in the invisible
part of the world.

In this system of cosmological conceptions it was not easy to account for the existence of the moon unless he was present as the god Thoth in the barque of the sun-god. The task became much simpler when the universe was interpreted as one universal god: then the sun and moon became the two eyes of this god, the sun the right eye, the moon the left. But the part played by the moon in the remote primitive periods of Egyptian civilization was an important one, for the easily observable moon phases served to divide time into units of approximately equal length, the month. Later it was recognized that time could be much more precisely measured with the help of the sun in years, with which the lunar months could not be brought into agreement. The calculation in lunar months was, therefore, given up for practical purposes and retained solely in the cult for festivals and offerings connected with the changes of the moon. The original importance of the moon is, however, reflected by the myth according to which the sun-god appointed Thoth, the moon-god, as his deputy in the sky by night, and Thoth is called *"Rē that shines in the night"* and the *"representative"* of Rē or of Atum. He is also called *"reckoner of time"*.

Another conception which also seems to have existed was of a universal sky-god called simply Wēr (*"the Great One"*), with special emphasis on his aspect as the god of light, later identified with Horus. The sun and moon were his eyes, and he bore the epithet of Mekhenti-irty (*"He on whose forehead are the Two Eyes"*); on moonless nights or during an eclipse he became Mekhenti-en-irty (*"He on whose forehead there are no eyes"*). In this latter aspect popular phantasy made him the protector of the blind, the doctor of those with eye-diseases and the patron of musicians, who were often blind; he was even imagined as a harp-playing god. This fate of his is a good example of how a universal deity elaborated by theologians could in popular belief fall back into the anthropomorphic stage.

Just as men and the organic world were created by a god and contained something of his divine substance, so inanimate objects were considered as a part of the body of a god, or as having emanated from his body. This was especially the case with the flood waters of the Nile which were sometimes, as

we have seen, believed to have come from Nun, or were called
the limbs of Osiris or even the sweat coming forth from his
dead body. The air was called *"limbs of Amun"*, flint and iron
came forth from the body of Sētekh. The Egyptian word for
incense, *sonter*, means simply *"divine odour"*.

Man may be subject to fate or *"destiny"* (Egyptian *Shoy*
from *sho* "to destine") which is laid down for him by seven
goddesses, Hathors, at his birth. It may be *"bad"* and concern
his misfortunes, the length of his life and the kind of death he
will die, or it may be *"good"*; it is then called "destiny"—
Renenet, this being the name of the goddess of nursing who
assists the child at birth and protects it. In her connection
with destiny Renenet was early interpreted as the personification of *"riches"* and *"fortune"*, as she became confused with
Ernutet, another goddess of similar name. Ernutet, however,
was originally a personification of the harvest in the form of a
cobra or a cobra-headed woman, since the cobra was often
found in the ripe corn. The fusion of the two goddesses was
favoured by the fact that in Egypt the harvest was the foundation
of riches. As the real creators of man, Amun, Ptah and Khnum
are also sometimes called *"destiny"*.

One's destiny is not inescapable, man can change it through
his own actions and effort *"if the god will"*, since *"the morrow
is in the hand of the god"*. The child is born with the acquiescence
of the gods; when parents pray to them the gods *"order that it
should be born"* to them; and from then onwards man can do
things only with divine approval, he proposes, the god disposes,
or—as an Egyptian sage puts it—*"the words which man says
are one thing, the things which God doeth are another"*.

A good example of what the Egyptian hoped to obtain from
his god is the list of favours which King Ramesses IV demands
from Osiris as a reward for all the pious acts that he has done
for the god. He claims them both for himself and on behalf
of his subjects, whose spokesman he is. In true Egyptian fashion
they are expressed in a very concrete way:

*"And thou shalt give me health, life and old age, a long reign,
strength to all my limbs; sight to my eyes, hearing to my ears and
pleasure to my heart daily. And thou shalt give me to eat to
satiety, and thou shalt give me to drink to drunkenness, and thou*

shalt promote my seed to be kings in this country to eternity and for ever. And thou shalt make me content every day, thou shalt listen to my voice in whatever I shall say to thee and grant me very high Nile floods to furnish thy offerings and to furnish the offerings of the gods and goddesses, the lords of Northern and Southern Egypt, to preserve the sacred bulls, to preserve all the people of thy land, their cattle and their trees which thy hand has made. For it is thou who hast made them all, thou canst not abandon them to pursue another design with them, for that would not be right."

Here we find first the things which an Egyptian valued most: life and health until a ripe old age, plenty of food and drink and the same station in life for his children as he had himself; then high Nile floods, on which depends the welfare of the inhabitants of the country and their chief possessions, flocks and trees, as well as the offerings brought to the gods. And at the end comes the argument which cannot fail to move the god to fulfil the king's wishes: The god created all these beings and thus has assumed an obligation to care for them; he has no right to change the plans which he had when creating the world.

There is no document earlier than the New Kingdom setting forth systematically the ideas that Egyptians had formed about their gods. The picture of the character of the gods must be laboriously fitted together from more recent allusions. For the Old and Middle Kingdom there are hardly more than proper names to give us a glimpse into the beliefs of the common people and their relationship with the gods. A considerable number of Egyptian proper names at all periods are theophorous, that is, they contain some statement concerning a deity. Given by the father shortly after birth when the child was brought to him, these theophorous names show the impact of religion on the life of an Egyptian. A name containing the name of a god was certainly given because the child was considered by its parents to be a gift of the gods, and the god's name must have been thought to bring luck.

In the Old Kingdom a god is said to "*abide*" or to "*appear* (like the sun)". Gods "*live*" (or "*belong to life*", are "*lords of life*"), they are "*great*", "*powerful*" and "*strong*", "*good*" ("beautiful"), *"merciful"*, *"noble"*, *"high"* and *"just"*. Like men they have a *ka* or several *kas* and these also are powerful, good, pure, great, noble and abiding. Their *bais* (external manifestations) *"appear* (like the sun)" and are *"great"* and *"good"*. They *"make"* or *"bring"* a child, *"love it"*, *"bring it up"*, *"protect"* it while they stand *"behind"* it, *"keep it alive"* or *"nourish"* it, *"clothe"* it, and *"make it healthy"*, *"favour"* it, *"come"* to it, *"lift it up"*, in short *"its life is in the hand of the god"*, for man is his *"servant"* and *"adores"* the god. Most of the foregoing statements concern Ptah, but this is undoubtedly accidental: the majority of proper names of that period—in fact the majority of surviving monuments of the Old Kingdom in general—come from the region of Memphis; it is, therefore, only natural to find the god of the capital appearing so often in proper names. Judging from some names containing the names of other gods, the same characteristics apply to them also, and apply to any god, in fact to gods in general.

The Middle Kingdom names have little to add to this picture. The gods are also *"sweet"* and *"pleasant"*, people are their *"sons"* and *"daughters"* and the gods *"make them good"*. For the first time we hear that gods are *"in festival"* and though they are said to be in the *"columned hall"* or in the *"courtyard"* of the temple, they also appear in public *"on the lake"* or *"navigating"* on the Nile. If anything can be inferred from the absence of names of this latter type in earlier periods, their appearance in the Middle Kingdom would testify a closer contact of the deities with the common folk, a contact which would be entirely in agreement with the democratization of religious ideas that we seem to perceive in the social upheaval between the Old and Middle Kingdoms.

The prayers—or "hymns", as they are usually called by Egyptologists—down to the end of the Middle Kingdom are singularly void of any reference to the relation between the worshipper and his god. They consist mostly of rather tedious descriptions of the external form in which he appeared in statues and on reliefs, especially of his crowns and sceptres, of his might and of honours given to him by other gods and by humans at various places. They are full of mythological references which make them hardly intelligible to the modern reader without a lengthy commentary. Nevertheless, even at the risk of adding very little information as to the nature of the god, two examples should be quoted in full here; they will also show how the information supplied by the seemingly inexhaustible wealth of Egyptian religious texts shrinks as soon as the religious feelings of the ancient Egyptians are investigated. The two prayers which follow are, one to the rising sun, pronounced in the morning, and one to the god Min-Horus.

"Adoration of Rē when he rises in the eastern horizon of heaven with his followers.

Hail to thee Harakhte, Khepri who hast created thyself. How beautiful it is when thou arisest on the horizon and lightenest the Two Lands (=Egypt) with thy rays. All gods rejoice when they see thee as the King of all heaven, while the royal cobra is established on thy head and the crowns of South and North are on their apex, having established their seat on thy front. Thoth abides on the prow of thy boat punishing all thine enemies. Those who are in the Netherworld come forth at thy approach to see this beautiful apparition."

"I adore Min and exalt Horus who lifteth up (his) arms. Hail to thee, Min-at-his-appearings, with lofty plumes, son of Osiris, born of divine Isis, great in the Senut-sanctuary, mighty in Ipu, thou of Koptos, Horus, who lifteth up his arm, lord of respect, who hath silenced pride, ruler of all gods, rich in perfume, when he cometh down from the land of Medjau, respected in Nubia, thou of the land of Uteret."

It is only in the New Kingdom that we meet with prayers referring to the personal feelings of individuals towards divinities. To them we shall return in the next chapter.

The mysterious power which enabled gods to accomplish actions beyond the ability of man was *hike*, "magic, magical power". The possession of this magical power was by no means restricted to the gods, certain mortals also, the magicians, had it and were, therefore, supposed to do things which otherwise only gods could do; but gods—and the king with them—possessed *hike* in a higher degree than anyone else. Of course if a magician had succeeded in acquiring more *hike* than a god, he could then have commanded a god to come to his service and help. Magicians often believed or pretended that they had gained a greater knowledge of this mysterious art than a god. The god was not then implored to comply with the wishes of a human being, but was forced to abandon his detachment and was induced into co-operation.

But not only the gods and the living were in need of magic; the dead were believed to need it even more, and Egyptian funerary literature—especially the Pyramid texts, the inscriptions on the coffins of the Middle Kingdom and the Book of the Dead—consisted to a great extent of magic spells which, devised originally for the use of the living, were introduced into tombs for the benefit of the dead. Owing to the supernatural character of the world of the gods and the dead, all actions in their two worlds, and any contact made by the living with them, took place through *hike*. Thus any religious act would be magic from the Egyptian point of view; indeed the Egyptian language had no word for "religion"; *hike* was the nearest approach to it.

From the modern standpoint, however, we can apply the term "magic" only to such actions by the living as were performed for the benefit of the living, either the magician himself or other persons, and were of so difficult a nature as to require the use of a supernatural power. Gods and the dead might be invoked and their help sought in such magical actions but, properly speaking, these actions do not come within the scope of a study of Egyptian religion.

Magical power manifested itself through deed or word; the efficacy of this power could be tested by anyone in the visible world, but parallel to this it was effective in an imaginary, supernatural world which was, however, no less real. The magic of gods (and of magicians) was so powerful that it had an effect not only in the supernatural world, but also in the visible one. Thus the god Khnum made a human figure on a potters-wheel and so created Man. But speech, especially an order couched in words, also had a magic power; to pronounce words was to evoke in the supernatural world the things which they designated; this is why good words (*e.g.*, blessings) are to be recommended, and evil words (*e.g.*, curses) should be avoided by all well-meaning people. Names, in particular, were closely connected with the substance of the thing or person named; the knowledge of their name gave one power over them: the god Ptah created the things of the visible world simply by naming them.

The magic power of speech and action was also shared by writing. This belief is by no means restricted to ancient Egypt: let us remember that the word "grammar" (learning, knowledge of writing) is at the root of the English "glamour", the original meaning of which is "enchantment" and of the French *grimoire* (=book of magic spells). The hieroglyphs consisting of images of living beings and inanimate objects were more imbued with potential magic than any other kind of writing, since, in addition to the existence and power of the words they expressed, the individual figures of human beings and animals they represented were also capable of assuming a mysterious existence.

Both the deities dwelling or manifested in objects and animals, and the gods who are personifications of natural phenomena and are manifested in the phenomena themselves, underwent at a relatively early date a personification in human form; but besides these two classes there are a number of divinities who are personifications in human form of certain abstract conceptions or activities. Analogy on the original fetishes and animal and nature gods played its part here and underlying human characters were added to the abstract nouns of the language which made it possible to treat them on the same footing as other deities in pictorial art or in myths. In representations they were usually provided with certain marks which made them at once recognizable to an Egyptian.

We have already met personifications of Shoy *"Fate"* as a man and of Renenet *"Nursing"* as a woman, and may add here personifications of certain materials, like Napri *"Corn"* as a god, Nub *"Gold"* as a goddess (because for some reason or other *"Gold"* became early an epithet or attribute of the goddess Hathor), Kebhōwet *"Cold Water Libation"* as a goddess, and activities such as *"Weaving"* (the goddess Tayet) and *"Wine-pressing"* (the god Shesmu). Certain conceptions of time are found personified in the goddesses Ronpet *"Year"*, Akhet *"Flood-season"* and Proyet *"Spring"* and the god Shomu *"Summer"*, the sex of the deity being decided by the gender of the Egyptian words. There are also geographical conceptions such as the goddess Sokhet *"Cultivable Plain"*, the god Ha *"Desert"* and the goddess Amentet *"West"*, who bear on their heads hieroglyphic signs for "field", "desert" and "west" respectively.

The most important among all the personifications, however, is Ma'et, personifying both *"Right"* and *"Truth"*, for which Egyptian had only one word. Ma'et is a goddess whose name appears as early as the IInd Dynasty; very early too she is represented bearing on her head an ostrich feather which for some unknown reason had become her symbol. She is *"daughter of Rē"*, for Rē, the sun-god, rules the universe according to the principles of *"right"* and *"justice"* (both *ma'et*) which he has laid down, and Ma'et is, therefore, regularly seen standing on the prow of the sun-barque accompanying the sun-god on his course across the sky.

The most conspicuous attribute of a god was his power; thus gods are sometimes referred to as *sekhem "powers"* and are then represented materialized in a sceptre of a special form also called *sekhem* (lit. *"powerful one"*). Osiris is a *sekhem* or *sekhem ō, "power"* or *"great power"*, and at the same time also a *"sekhem-sceptre"* or *"great sekhem-sceptre"*, since despite his entirely human nature he was given the material form of a sceptre in his temple at Abydos. A large *sekhem*-sceptre was kept there in a shrine and carried through the town in religious processions. A golden cap with a human face was placed over the top of the sceptre to recall the original human form of the god. The sceptre thus ended in a head, emphasized by the cap bearing two high feathers as a crown and two cobras above the face; it was inlaid with blue faience or precious stones and tied with ribbons as if it were a wig.

Had the ancient Egyptians been more logical and consistent than they were they could have put in order the multitude of gods with which they were faced when the political union of the country was achieved. It would certainly have been possible to define the character of each of the various gods more clearly and to delimit his sphere of action and influence in relation to the others, as the Greeks did in their pantheon. The Egyptians never attempted this course and were unable to do so. Their conception of their local gods was too universal, and when the god of a temporary capital attained political preponderance, the only course they saw open to them was to identify the others with him so that they could all keep their universal character. Only a few smaller divinities were assigned special spheres and to them personifications of some abstract ideas were added later.

Among the important gods there were two who while never attaining the grade of supreme universal god but remaining of secondary rank, were worshipped everywhere throughout the country. They were Thoth and Anubis. Expressed in terms of human society, their relation to the supreme god can be said to have been that of the highest official, the vizier, to the king. Thoth was in the realm of the god of the living, the sun-god, while Anubis was under Osiris in the realm of the dead; Thoth, however, also penetrates into the kingdom of Osiris and becomes associated with Anubis, as we shall see presently.

Thoth whom we have already met as the moon-god was also the god of wisdom and learning. This is explained by his connexion with the moon, since the moon impressed the ancient Egyptians by its changes. As moon-god Thoth is called "*Lord of Heavens*", "*Mysterious*", "*Unknown*", "*Silent One*", "*Beautiful of the Night*" and so forth. The greatest festival of Thoth was celebrated in the first month of the Egyptian calendar and from the New Kingdom onwards the first month itself was called Thoth. The grave appearance of the ibis was probably the reason why this bird was considered as another personification of Thoth (he is often directly spoken of as "*Ibis*"), the same may be true of the baboon, whose connexion with Thoth ("*great and august Baboon*") dates from much later times.

As the god of wisdom Thoth received the epithet "*the Knowing One*", "*skilled in knowledge*"; it was from books that he derived his learning and power as "*great in magic*" or "*lord of magic*". He was the inventor of writing and the author of the traditional law and order set forth in sacred books. Being himself an "*excellent scribe*" he was the patron of scribes; in the New Kingdom a seated statue of his baboon was set up in many offices, for he "*gave offices to whom he loved*", "*made great him who was skilled in his employment*" and "*promoted to positions*". He was "*scribe*" or "*letter-writer*" of the gods and "*scribe

of accounts" of the sun-god. According to the myth he recon-
ciled the two fighting brother gods, Horus and Sētekh, and
by his magic healed the eye of Horus which had been injured
in the fighting, so that it was again *"healthy"* (udjat) eye. He
distinguished the tongues of different countries; perhaps for
this reason he was also *"lord of foreign lands"* as early as the
Old Kingdom.

As a scribe Thoth accompanied the sun-god into the underworld and there noted down on his writing palette the results
of the weighing of the hearts of the dead. He did it conscienti-
ously, for he *"loved truth"* and *"falsehood was his abomination"*.

Anubis, on the contrary, who usually attends to the balance
at the judgment of the deceased always remained a god exclusively concerned with the dead; as such we shall have the
opportunity of saying more about him in the next chapter.

It has been seen that the Egyptians had arrived at a conception of a universal god without being able to give up the
others who had been bequeathed to them from the past.
According to the locality or the momentary political constella-
tion this supreme god appeared under various names, while
the other gods were considered as different aspects of the same
divine personality. Only once in Egyptian history a remarkable
attempt was made to introduce a true monotheism while dis-
carding all the other numerous gods and their worship. If such
an attempt was to have any chance of success at all, even if
only a temporary one, it had to come from no less a person
than the highest authority in the country who was in a position
to enforce such a change, namely the king himself. And indeed
it was Amenhotep IV of the XVIIIth Dynasty who earned the
fame of being the only reformer and heretic in the history of
Egypt.

Unfortunately very little is known about the youth of the
king and the impulses which led him to his religious reform.
His portraits seem to indicate that he was delicate of body and
of uncertain health and was, therefore, not predestined for
military deeds. This seems to have led him to concentrate on
thinking and dreaming. The universal god at that time was
Amon-Rē, who combined in his personality Amun, the local
god of Thebes, then the capital, with the old Heliopolitan sun-

god, Rē. In Rē himself, however, three different conceptions of the sun-god were blended: that of the celestial body (Rē, *"Sun"*), of the falcon (Horus) and of the falcon-headed man (Rē-Harakhte, *"Rē-Horus of the Horizon"*). There must for some time have been religious circles which laid more stress on the purely material character of the sun-god as a sun-disk, Aton, for this word is mentioned with increasing frequency in the reign of Amenhotep III, the father and predecessor of Amenhotep IV. This was the conception of the sun-god which Amenhotep IV accepted and thought out in all its aspects. But it was only gradually that he put his ideas into effect. Indeed, shortly after his appointment as co-regent to his old and sick father, he still undertook buildings for Amon-Rē and his monuments of that time give no indication of what is to come.

Soon after, however, we see the king serving a new god with a strange long name which reads in translation *"Lives Rē-Harakhte of the two horizons, who rejoices in the horizon in his name of Show, who is the Aton"*. It is not easy to understand this definition which is the centre of the king's teaching. It states that Show (an old god of the air and light) is only another name of Rē-Harakhte and that this latter is also the sun-disk. Rē-Harakhte points to Heliopolis as the origin of Amenhotep IV's idea; all its elements are old, it is only the formulation that is new. There is also pictorial evidence that even at this stage the new god was in falcon-headed human form.

Nothing would have happened probably if the problem had been only to introduce a new god equal to the others: the Egyptian religion has proved very hospitable and many a new god had been accepted from abroad into the Egyptian pantheon. The matter was complicated by the complete omission of the god Amun from the name of the new god; for Amun Amenhotep IV had no use, and this undoubtedly caused great dissatisfaction among Amun's priests. And when in his fifth or sixth regnal year the king made preparations for his "thirty years jubilee"—a festival the true nature of which is still obscure to us—he had abandoned the original anthropomorphic form of Aton, as his new god was also called for short, and began to represent him as the celestial body itself, in the form of a sun-disk from which rays come down ending in hands. Each hand holds the hieroglyphic sign for "life" which it tenders to the nose of the king or the members of his family—his Queen Nofretete and several daughters, for Amenhotep IV had no son. The god celebrated the "thirty years festival" together with the king and was now called *"Aton, the living, the great, who is in thirty years festivals"*, for the god is the supreme lord, a king himself. His full name is divided into two cartouches as a true royal name.

At last Amenhotep IV decided to build a new residence for the god and himself. He chose for it a place hitherto unclaimed by any deity or human being, about half-way between Thebes and Memphis, near the present village of Amarna in Middle Egypt. Its name was to be *"Horizon of the Aton"* (Akhetaton). It is almost certain that the stimulus which led the king to this decision was the growing resistance of the priesthood of Amun to his god, to which the king retaliated by the persecution of the cult of Amun and his clergy. Even the memory of Amun had to be wiped out and on all monuments the figures and name of Amun began to be fanatically effaced. The king went so far as to give up his name Amenhotep since it contained the name of Amun ("Amun is content") and adopted a new name Ekhnaton "It pleases Aton".

But Ekhnaton's zeal did not stop at Amun: the king also repudiated the other gods, though his persecution of them was less systematic than in the case of Amun. Their temples were abolished and sanctuaries of Aton were constructed in various towns of Egypt. Thus Aton was no more *unus inter pares*, but the only god and consequently the plural *"gods"* is found effaced now and then in inscriptions. The queen too changed her name to Nefer-nefru-Aton ("Beautiful is the Beauty of Aton") and, needless to say, the names of all of Ekhnaton's daughters also contained the name of his god.

In Ekhnaton's sixth year the area of the new residence was delimited by means of a series of huge stelae covered with inscriptions and the work on building a vast town was carried on very actively. Nothing was forgotten, from several sanctuaries for Aton, palaces for the king and his family, and spacious villas for his important adherents, down to tombs for the king and his followers in the hills east of the town. The main temple of Aton consisted of several courtyards with altars in the open air, thus recalling the sun-temples of the Vth Dynasty, while the traditional temples of the old gods invariably housed the images of these divinities in dark sanctuaries.

Into this new town Ekhnaton moved with his family, never to leave it again according to a pledge he had made in his foundation decree. There he went on dreaming and contemplating; he paid no attention to the events in the Egyptian possessions in Syria and Palestine, which were on the verge of collapsing under incessant attacks by foreign enemies. In about the tenth year of his reign Ekhnaton also dropped Horus from the name of the new god so that the final form of the name reads: "*Lives Rē, ruler of the two horizons, rejoicing in the horizon in his name of Rē, the father who has come (again) as Aton*". Thus the last tie still connecting the new religion with the old disappears; it even seems almost as if the words "who has come as Aton" imply a re-establishment of the sun-god's unlimited reign on earth interrupted since his mythical retirement to heaven.

The king points out in his inscriptions that his new teaching comes from his father Aton, as if it were a revelation of which he himself were only a prophet. The simple contents of the new creed are set forth best in a hymn to Aton of which two versions—a fuller and a shortened one—are known, composed by the king himself. It is a poem in praise of the sun and its blessings, which are light and life, love and truth, and is couched in simple but moving words.

Ekhnaton must have had many faithful adherents who shared his religious idea, and not only in the residence but elsewhere, otherwise his orders could not have been executed as efficiently as they were; on the other hand a number of these followers were won over by the prospect of a brilliant career at court and in the administration; nor did the king shrink from bribing others by rich gifts to ensure their support. There were circles in the country where he was considered as a madman and others where he was hated. And for the lower classes of the population his ideas seem to have been too lofty to prevent them from clinging to their old beliefs. In the workmen's village in the vicinity of the residence proofs were found that the inhabitants of the village had by no means discarded their old divinities, great and small, such as the hippopotamus-goddess Toëris and the gods Bes and Shed, or Hathor and Isis. Probably neither the king nor the circle round him paid any attention to the religious views of these people.

It is sometimes suggested that Ekhnaton's endeavour was to create a religion which, stripped of all purely Egyptian features, especially the mythology, would be acceptable to all peoples of the Egyptian empire. Indeed it is possible that Ekhnaton realized the international character of his god, but it is not likely that he was a man whose ideas were inspired by practical political needs; on the contrary he appears rather to have been driven by purely religious fanaticism. There are no proofs that he ever tried to introduce his religion to peoples outside Egypt except for naming a town in Nubia Gematon after the new god and building a temple to him there. The king does not show on his monuments any concern for non-Egyptians, indeed he is entirely absorbed by his own relation to Aton and does not show concern for anybody except himself and members of his family.

The way in which Ekhnaton insisted on calling himself "King who lives in Truth" shows that he attached much importance to the "Truth". It is quite possible that "Truth" is here to be understood as what we call "reality" and that Ekhnaton considered himself and wanted to be considered a realist. Indeed, the only two unrealistic things about the appearance of his god are the cobra and the rays which end in hands clasping the sign for life, but the hands are probably only an expression of a poetical figure and the cobra was a common symbol of royalty. The king's realism is further manifested in the impetus which he gave to Egyptian art, especially the way in which he had his portraits executed both in painting and sculpture. In the inscriptions of his reign the spoken idiom has been introduced into the writing and the earlier language which was no more spoken and was hardly understood is discarded entirely.

Ekhnaton's death after seventeen years' reign was the beginning of the end of his religion. The author who would enforce it disappeared and the forces of the reaction were loosed. His

E

second successor, Tutankhaton ("Living image of Aton")
marked an open return to the old religion by changing his
name into Tutankhamun, "Living image of Amun". He is also
known to have returned to Thebes, where he was buried. Under
Tutankhamun's successor, Haremhab, a persecution of the
memory of Ekhnaton began and his name and portraits and
the name of his god, when written in the cartouches, were
destroyed wherever they were found. It is, however, interesting
to note that this hatred was directed principally against the
person of the author of Atonism and less against the god Aton
himself. It is true that his sun-disk with rays ending in hands
was never represented again, but it was everywhere left intact.
Ekhnaton however went down into Egyptian history as *the
enemy of Akhetaton*" and his reign was referred to as the years
"of the Rebel".

CHAPTER III

MEN AND THE GODS

ACCORDING to the official view the king was the only mortal who was ever entitled to have direct contact with the gods. In fact, during the Old and Middle Kingdoms pictures of gods are totally absent from the monuments set up by ordinary men, and a common mortal is never represented in the act of worshipping a deity. Still, from their titles we see that people were often connected with a divinity as priests, and the names of gods are often mentioned in the inscriptions in tombs and on the stelae or statues. The absence of figures of the gods cannot, therefore, be explained by the people's indifference to the gods, nor can it be fully explained by the purpose of the decorations on the walls of tombs and other funerary monuments; the very existence of these was supposed to ensure the continued life both of the deceased, and of the necessary, and, therefore, desired, possessions which he had acquired in his earthly life. It is only at the beginning of the Second Intermediate Period that figures of gods appear on the monuments of private people, at first shyly, and then with increasing frequency as the New Kingdom progressed. During this period commoners are found figuring in the presence of deities, and lifting their arms to them in adoration or presenting them with offerings.

It seems that the absence of gods from private monuments is due to some kind of shyness, or to that official view which made the king, the son of a god and a god himself, the only representative of humans in the presence of the gods. This explanation is the more likely, as the king himself does not, in earlier periods, appear on private monuments or in the company of commoners, but is treated as if on the same footing as the gods. The change displayed from the Second Intermediate Period onwards is due to the absolute equality for all in religion which was achieved by the time of the XIIth Dynasty, and which required some time to become apparent in art. This democratization of religious conceptions was, however, never recognized officially. In theory every temple was built by the king and the king only, "*as his monument*" to a god, and the king continued to communicate with the god to the exclusion of everybody else.

The short interlude of heresy under Ekhnaton, despite the outward return to the old religion which followed, is generally accepted as the turning point which opened the Egyptian texts, on which our knowledge of the personal attitude of the Egyptians towards their gods is based, to a freer expression of feelings, hopes and fears, than had been possible or customary before. We possess a group of prayers of a new character dating from the time of the XIXth Dynasty; some of them are in manuscripts on papyrus and were copied in schools as part of the teaching of writing, but by far the larger number are a group of small stone stelae originally set up at and near the modern site called Der el-Medîneh in the Theban Necropolis. During the New Kingdom this place was occupied by a village and cemetery for the workmen engaged in carving the royal tombs in the rocks of the Valley of Kings. As royal workmen they were, no doubt, rather privileged among the working class, but only as far as their material situation was concerned; they were better and more regularly paid than was usual, and their relative wealth enabled them to have these stelae made and set up in their tombs and in the sanctuaries of various divinities situated in the village. But we can safely assume that their education and outlook did not differ much from those of the rest of the working and peasant population; consequently the small monuments which they left represent the spirit of the labouring and peasant classes whose poverty prevented them from displaying their religious feelings in this relatively costly way.

In these inscriptions the humility of the worshipper before his god and his appeal for mercy, as well as the confession of his weaknesses and sins, contrast remarkably with the self-assured tone and the assumption of infallibility pervading all the earlier religious literature. The evidence collected from earlier theophorous proper names, which we have already quoted, suggests that these sentiments were not new or peculiar to the New Kingdom; what is new is their open admission, and the impulse which led to their disclosure in writing. This change of attitude appears immediately after the close of Atonism, and it is difficult not to see in it one of the permanent results of the Amarna period.

Practically all the major gods are represented among those for whom these stelae were erected: Amun and Amon-Rē, Rē-Harakhte, Ptah, Thoth and Isis, besides a certain number of smaller deities whose worship was peculiar to the working class of the Theban Necropolis. Here Amun is *"that beloved God who hearkens to humble entreaties, who stretches forth his hand to the humble, who saves the weak"*, *"who hears prayer, comes at the voice of the distressed humble one, who gives breath to him that is wretched"*, and Rē-Harakhte is called *"august, beloved, merciful God who hears him that prays, who hears the humble entreaties of him that calls upon him, who comes at the voice of him that utters his name."* Prayers are addressed to God in order to mitigate his power and wrath which have stricken the suppliant in consequence of some misdeed. Thus a man confesses on his stela to Thoth: *"I am that man who uttered an oath falsely by the Moon (i.e., Thoth) . . . And he caused me to see the greatness of his power before the whole land. . . . Be ye ware of the Moon. O merciful one, that art able to turn this (affliction) away"*. Similarly the sculptor Ken was the man *"who uttered an oath falsely"* to a woman, and now prays *"to Show and all gods of heaven and earth"*, more particularly to the Moon-Thoth, Ptah and Amun, *"Be merciful to me"*. In a few cases Thoth has inflicted upon the worshipper a *"darkness of his (the god's) making"*, by which perhaps some affection of the sight or blindness is meant: *"Lighten me"* or *"be merciful to me that I may see thee (again)"*. That this explanation is correct is made almost certain by another workman's stela to Ptah, where he says: *"I am a man who swore falsely to Ptah, Lord of Truth, and he caused me to behold darkness by day. . . . He caused me to be as a dog of the street while I was in his hand. He caused men and gods to mark me, I being as a man who has wrought abomination against his Lord. Righteous was Ptah, Lord of Truth, towards me when he chastised me. Be merciful to me so that I may see thy mercy"*. The draughtsman Nebrē—to quote a last example —dedicates a large stela to Amon-Rē on behalf of his son, the draughtsman Nekhtamun "*who lay sick unto death, who was under the might of Amun*" apparently because of a certain misbehaviour of his, and the father promised to the god: "*I will make this memorial in thy name and establish for thee this hymn in writing upon it, if thou doest save the draughtsman Nekhtamun for me.*" He was confident that "*though the servant is disposed to do evil, yet the Lord is disposed to be merciful*", for man sins because he is (as still another stela puts it) "*ignorant and foolish, who knows neither good nor evil*".

Clearly these people did not dare—or perhaps were not allowed—to approach the great state gods in their temples across the river in the town of Thebes, with their troubles and confessions, but felt more confident and at ease while facing them in the smaller sanctuaries of which even small towns or villages had several. Statues of the great gods set up in these sanctuaries were no less the seats of the divinities than those in the great temples in which their cult had originated. The small sanctuaries became in some way branches of the principal ones, and their deities developed in time into new local gods, differentiated from the original ones by a local epithet often referring to some special aspect of the god, or to the place of his new seat.

Thus besides "*Amun of Opet-rīset* (Luxor)" or "*Amon-Rē, King of the Gods, Lord of the Thrones of the Two Lands*" at Karnak, on the Theban West side we find "*Amun of the Happy Encounter*" (both the exact position of his sanctuary, and the significance of his epithet being still unknown), and "*Amun of Pakhenty*", Pakhenty being the name of a small village in that region; a small sanctuary in the Valley of Queens was the seat of "*Ptah in the Place of Beauty*". The temple of the local goddess Sakhmet of Memphis had a branch in an old funerary temple at Abusîr, and the goddess was called there "*Sakhmet of Sahurē*" after the royal builder of the temple in the Vth Dynasty. A number of votive stelae were found in small niches hacked out of the walls of the temple among the beautiful original reliefs; some of these small stelae bore, besides prayers, pictures of one or several human ears, undoubtedly symbolizing the ears of the deity which were believed to hear the petitions of the suppliant. The custom was not limited to this particular sanctuary, but is met with in other temples, especially the temple of Ptah at Memphis.

Besides these new forms of old gods, the belief and phantasy of the common people created a series of smaller divinities who attained great popularity among all classes, although they had no official recognition. How intimately connected they were with the people is shown by the fact that they had no sanctuaries of their own, but had their seats of worship in the home; this is quite an unusual feature for an Egyptian deity, since in Egypt the dignity of a god required that he should have his own *"house"* or *"castle"*, that is a temple or shrine of his own. How near these smaller gods stood to the common people can further be seen from the appearance of some of them: they do not have a lofty and dignified attitude but rather a grotesque shape conforming to the Egyptian sense of humour and a satirical streak in the Egyptian mind. It is these traits which make Egyptian popular stories and tales of even the great gods represent them with weaknesses derived from humans and place them in situations which cannot but be called ridiculous.

Toëris (graecized form of the Egyptian Twēret *"The Great One"*), was one of the smaller divinities; she was a domestic goddess represented as a pregnant hippopotamus standing on her hind-legs, and usually leaning against the hieroglyphic sign for "Protection". Everything suggests that votive statuettes of Toëris were believed to ensure protection to mothers in childbirth and to babies. She is the only one from this category of divinities for whom in later times a temple was built at Karnak.

Another purely domestic god was Bēs, a bandy-legged dwarf with broad face, wide mouth with protruding tongue, a beard resembling a lion's mane and an animal's ears and tail. He danced and played the lute for the merriment of the gods, but was supposed to contribute to happiness and good temper in human households as well. His figure or face could often be seen in relief or painting on walls of houses, beds and head rests, mirror-handles and perfume boxes, and on pottery. Other dwarf-like figures resembled Bēs, into whom the phantasy of the people transformed some of the great gods, especially Ptah and Rē. Rē is *"that dwarf, someone who is in Heliopolis, the short one whose legs are between sky and earth"*; but although a dwarf he is, nevertheless, one *"of millions of cubits"*—for such un-doubtedly is the distance between the sky and the earth—and his figure appears sketched beside the text of magic spells written on a piece of papyrus, folded and worn on the body as a powerful talisman. He is probably identical with the dwarf often pictured crouching on the prow of the sun-boat, once described as the *"dwarf with large face, tall back and short thighs"*. Another creature called Aha (*"Fighter"*), very much like Bēs, appears in the company of Toëris and various fabulous monsters on magical knives which are usually cut from hippo-potamus tusks and were believed to destroy hostile demons.

Shed (*"Saviour"*), originally perhaps a personification of the tutelary aspect of the god Onuris of This, was a young prince who hunted gazelles and lions in the desert in his chariot drawn by two horses; he also pursued snakes, scorpions and crocodiles. Small plaquettes bearing his image and hung round the neck were, therefore, considered as potent. magic against these dangerous creatures. Shed, too, is called *"great god, lord of heaven"*, and *"lord of deserts"* and was soon identified with the young Horus (Hor-Shed). He is then found represented on stelae as a divine child, standing naked on the heads of two crocodiles and holding in his hands snakes and scorpions and a lion and a gazelle, while the rest of the surface of the stone is covered by protective magic spells. These stone stelae are too large and heavy to be worn on the body, so they were probably set up in the houses as a protection.

The creation of the goddess Merseger on the West side of Thebes was an attempt to propitiate the deadly cobra. She had the form of a cobra or of a woman with either a human or a snake's head, and was called *"Mistress of the West"*, in other words, of the Necropolis, and more especially the Necropolis of Thebes, a function suited to her name (*"She who loves silence"*). Her particular seat was the mountain peak which towers to a height of more than 1,000 ft. over the Valley of Kings and the surrounding country, and Mertseger was also called the *"Peak"* (Ta-dehnet in Egyptian, Kurn with the same meaning being the modern Arabic name of the mountain). The slope of the Peak was covered with numberless tiny shrines, each built of a few stones and sheltering an inscribed stela dedicated to one or more tutelary divinities, Mertseger among them. Since the goddess Hathor had an important sanctuary at Dêr el-Bahari, which was close by under the cliffs, Mertseger was often thought to be only another aspect of Hathor.

The example of the Peak shows how even at a relatively late stage of the Egyptian religion—almost all the popular divinities quoted are of the New Kingdom—inanimate objects, in this case a mountain, became the seats of a divine force and were consequently deified. Various ancient monuments, statues and buildings, objects connected with the cult, and trees were also deified in the same way. The famous Great Sphinx at Gîza was probably early interpreted as an image of the sun-god, though originally it was no more than a rock of peculiar shape cut and completed by the builder of Chephren's pyramid to resemble a crouching lion with the king's head, the symbol of royal power; it was then imitated on a smaller scale, and sphinxes of this kind often flanked the roads leading to temples.

An interesting list of Theban divinities of this order is contained in a letter whose sender commends its recipient to the Theban triad of Amun, Mut and Khons, and beside these to the "*Spirit in the Cedar, the love of Thebes, on the road of rams, to Amenhotep of the Forecourt, to Amenhotep the favourite, to Hathor of the Persea-tree, to Amun of Opet, to the eight apes who are in the Forecourt, to Hathor dwelling at Thebes, to the Great Gate of Baki, and to the gods and goddesses, lords of the City* (of Thebes)". Here the "*Spirit in (the) Cedar*" is the alley of crouching statues of the ram of Amun and "*Hathor of the Persea*" must have been some trees which were conspicuous by their age or size, or the place where they stood. The "*eight apes*" are, almost certainly, stone images of this animal, which was sacred to Thoth, standing in the courtyard of some temple, while the "*Great Gate of Baki*" may have been a temple pylon built by the High-priest of Amun, Bakenkhons, of whose name Baki would be a likely abbreviation.

"*Amenhotep of the Forecourt*" and "*Amenhotep, the favourite*" (namely of Amun, as is known from elsewhere), were two different statues of one and the same deified king, Amenhotep I, who, with his mother, the Queen Nefertari, enjoyed a special esteem and devotion throughout the country in general, and among the poorer class of the west of Thebes in particular. The reason for this popularity, which far surpassed that of the cult of any of the dead Pharaohs, was undoubtedly the fact that he had been the first king to be buried in a rock-hewn tomb at Thebes, and had organized the body of workmen who lived in the village of Der el-Medîneh and were engaged in the work on the tomb. Like the cults of other gods, his was not limited to its original and proper place, in his case his mortuary temple; several sanctuaries of his sprang up as branches of the original temple in settlements in the neighbourhood, each with its own statue of the king. Thus it gradually was almost forgotten that all these statues, most of which were also differentiated by details of attitude and dress, represented the same person, and a number of forms of the deified king were created (at least four others are known besides the two which have already been mentioned), each distinguished by a special epithet. The case of the Virgin Mary has been quoted as a not unfitting parallel to this division of the personality of one deity into various aspects. She is worshipped in varying external forms and with varying epithets ("of Lourdes", etc.) according to her alleged manifestation at different places.

Perhaps the oracles are the best illustrations of the interest which the deity was believed to take in human affairs. The oracles also show how the Egyptians almost forced their gods to abandon a passive attitude towards men and to reveal their will, advice or knowledge. This was done through the intermediary of the statue of the god which was asked questions, though more than one case is related where the initiative came from the god himself. Strangely enough, the practice of approaching the god and consulting him appears relatively late in Egypt, the first known instances dating from the New Kingdom. It is not necessary to conclude from this, as has sometimes been done, that the practice was originally foreign to Egypt, and was introduced from abroad; on the contrary, consultation with the god is the natural result of man's reasoning, and the rather original technique which the Egyptians devised for this purpose suggests that oracles in Egypt were of native origin.

The first reference to the divine will being manifested is probably that made by King Tuthmosis III, who relates how, when he was still a boy, the god Amun, in the course of a procession of his statue round the temple, noticed him and halted. Tuthmosis prostrated himself on the ground before the god, who thereupon led him to a part of the temple called "*Station of the King*", thereby publically recognizing him as king. In this case the god revealed his will unasked, but from now onwards cases multiply in which the revelation of a god's will was sought for by men. Nor are the cases restricted to those in which the king appears as petitioner in political matters; any Egyptian was able to address the god of his choice in purely personal matters. Since only the king and a few priests as his deputies had access to the sanctuary where the god rested, and which was his private home, this consultation with the god was reserved for his public appearances at festivals, when he made a tour of the temple and the town, although his statue was concealed within a portable shrine and hidden from view by a curtain. The shrine was mounted on a barque and this was carried on a litter. Many gods are attested as issuing oracles, and from this it seems that the practice was general with any deity.

The questions which the god was asked to answer never emanated from mere curiosity to learn the future; the wish to act in accordance with the god's will was usually at the root of the question. Often his help was sought in difficulty or uncertainty: a claim as to property was to be settled, the guilt of a person suspected of a crime had to be established, the god's approval of the appointment of an official had to be obtained, and so on, the god's function being that of judge. The questions were either presented orally, or were written on sherds or small pieces of papyrus in two forms, one affirmative and the other negative, and placed before the god when he was carried in procession. The god chose between the two by causing the bearers of his statue to walk towards the affirmative question to indicate "yes" (the god "*approved exceedingly*" say the texts) or towards the negative one to indicate "no". There seems to have been another procedure, when the petitioner read or recited his request; in this case the statue carried by the priests retreated to express disapproval; if it advanced, the reply was favourable.

Although the wish to see the matter settled by the god one way or the other may sometimes have made the bearers believe that the statue forced them to walk in the required direction, it is certain that no clever and deliberate deception was intended, and none can be assumed. The bearers of the statue of the god were always lay-priests (*wēeb*) who had undergone special purification beforehand, while the petitioners were in some cases members of a professional priesthood; these, if they had suspected unfair play, certainly would not have accepted a decision unfavourable to themselves. It is, therefore, safest to say that suggestion and auto-suggestion influenced the movements of the bearers.

The endeavour to act in accordance with the will of the gods is characteristic of the Egyptians; again and again they insist that a particular action taken was *"what the god has decreed"*. In the opinion of society, however, the standard of morals was set by men as well as gods: the standard was *"what men loved and what the gods approved"*, for that was *"good"* and *"just"*. The Egyptian uses the same word (*nūfer*) for both "good" and "beautiful", speaking, for instance, of a "good character" and of a thing or person "beautiful" to look at, and *nūfer* is further tinged with pleasantness and good luck. Of its two opposites, *djow* means both "bad" and "unpleasant, unlucky, sad", while *bōien* is "bad" often with a connotation of uselessness and disaster. These words have, therefore, both an aesthetic and a moral aspect. *Ma'* "true, right, just", and its substantive *ma'et* "truth, right, justice" belong, on the contrary, only to the ethical sphere. *Ma'et*, often personified as a goddess, has two opposite conceptions, *gōreg*, "lie, falsehood" and *yesfet* meaning approximately "wrong" and "sin". Sometimes a dual of *ma'et*, *ma'etey*, is found, but this dual form probably expresses only the full degree of the quality, and not the existence or conception of two truths or justices.

Responsibility for their actions fell entirely upon men themselves; for though the Egyptian believed in "fate", he did not assume that fate restricted the free will of an individual: rather fate was constituted by various happenings in the world around which influenced man's life from outside. Man had the opportunity of fighting and counteracting this influence by his own efforts.

What we call conscience was, according to the Egyptian, seated in the "heart" (*yeb*) which was also the seat of reason and desires. The voice of the heart was "*the voice of God*" and "*he whom it had led to a good course of action was happy*".

The practically minded Egyptians did not occupy themselves with theoretical speculation about an absolute good to be applied and followed under any circumstances and at all costs. Their point of view was purely utilitarian: it was desirable to do good because this was profitable to an individual, for the approval of gods and men sooner or later brought reward. To say the least, it assured one of a "*good name*" with one's contemporaries and with posterity, and it saved one's name from oblivion or malediction. The name was an important constituent of a thing or a person and contributed to their existence. A "good name" was remembered—the Egyptians thought—for ever, and its bearer enjoyed a prolonged life; such a name was something to be striven for.

Doing what is good and right corresponded to a great extent to good behaviour, and this was inculcated in young people by a special branch of literature called "*teachings*"; these were collections of maxims and admonitions setting forth practical wisdom—or better, cleverness—for life. These "teachings" were, or purported to be, the work of men who had themselves been successful in their lives and careers; there was, therefore, a certain guarantee of similar success for those who followed their advice. Parts of the translation of a late product of this literature, the "teaching of Amenemōpe", composed under the XXth or XXIst Dynasty, passed in a disfigured form into "The Proverbs" of the Old Testament. The oldest among the "teachings", that of Ptahhotep, a vizier of the Vth Dynasty, centres on behaviour towards one's superiors in various stations of life. The quintessence of the teaching is that though "*what has come to pass is the command of God*" and "*it is God who assigns the foremost place*", the best line to follow if one wants to advance is not to act in contradiction to the established order.

While in the Old Kingdom this order was based above all on a well-organized officialdom, the Middle Kingdom added service to the gods, that is religion, as part of the order. For though God created heaven and earth *"according to the desire"* of men, and plants and animals for their nourishment, he also meted out punishment, for *"he slays his enemies and punishes his children because of that which they devised when they were hostile"* and *"he has slain the refractory ones among them"*. It is impossible to escape him for *"God knows every name"*. *"More acceptable (to God) is the virtue of one that is just than the ox (as an offering) of him that worketh iniquity"*.

Experience has shown, however, that the divine order and its consequence, the reward of the good and the punishment of the wicked, are not always realized within this earthly life; and since the Egyptians had always believed in a continuation of life after death, it seemed to them quite natural, indeed demanded by logic, to extend or postpone the effects of the divine order (=justice) into the life beyond. It seems unlikely that this belief, namely that happiness in the life after death depends on the behaviour and actions during earthly life, existed as early as the Old Kingdom; otherwise we should almost certainly find it expressed in the written records of that period. Since, however, it is a current belief from the Middle Kingdom onward, we must conclude that it originated in that obscure period of Egyptian history called the First Intermediate Period, and in its chaotic and unsatisfactory political and social conditions, a vivid description of which is given by contemporary literary works.

A pessimistic outlook and the worthlessness of this life form the background of another piece of literature of about the same date, the "Dispute with his Soul of one who is tired of Life". Desperate at the hopeless condition of the world which he summarizes in the words *"There are none that are righteous, the earth is given over to the workers of iniquity"*, the man decides to commit suicide by throwing himself into the flames and tries to persuade his soul to follow him. The soul makes attempts to dissuade him from his decision and reminds him of the joys of life and the futility of the world of the dead from which there is no return; eventually, however, it yields to the last argument of the desperate man, that he who reaches the other world is in company with the gods, even himself like a god, and as such may work for the return of justice and peace in the earthly world.

The date of the composition of this and similar pessimistic literature shows, as we have already indicated, that pessimism concerning the earthly life was not the result of philosophic meditation but a reflection of historical events in contemporary literature. It is, moreover, in direct contradiction to the habitual optimistic attitude of the Egyptians to life and the enjoyment of its pleasures without any excessive fear of death, although death was something which an Egyptian never lost from sight making provision for it according to his means. Pessimism was not natural to an Egyptian, nor is there later, in the New Kingdom, a similar pessimism concerning the existence after death. The *carpe diem* attitude, too, is limited to a group of songs recited by harpists at festival meals, and is a complete antithesis to the conceptions which the Egyptians always had of the life after death. It is time now to set forth in some detail what these funerary conceptions were.

We can safely say that the Egyptians of the historical period always believed in immortality, though there is no word for immortality in their language. The same word *"life"* is used both for the earthly existence and for the existence after death. But immortality is not absolute; certain conditions have to be fulfilled to achieve it.

How far back the belief in life after death goes it is impossible to say. For prehistoric and early historic times the evidence for such a belief is purely archaeological, the graves of these periods containing food and various other equipment the presence of which would be inexplicable if life had not been imagined extending after death and under conditions very similar to life before death. The excellent state of preservation of dead bodies long after death, due to the extremely dry climate, may have largely contributed to the origin of the idea of continuity of life. The position in which the body was buried differed from place to place, but was fairly constant within the same cemetery, thus suggesting some variation or succession of funerary ideas.

Generally speaking the bodies faced east in historical times, while during the prehistoric period they lay on their left side, head south and facing west. It was the "West" which predominated as the land of the dead at all times down to the Coptic, where as *Amente* it still translates the Greek conception of Hades. The personified West, the goddess Amentet, is often represented welcoming the dead to her realm. There she also received the setting sun and no doubt it was the fact that the sun sets in the west which fostered this conception of the west as the world of the dead. Though many cemeteries were also situated east of the Nile, theoretically all the dead were buried *"in the beautiful West"* and *"departed to the West upon the beautiful roads on which the honoured ones* (=dead) *depart"*, as the inscriptions of the Old Kingdom often say; *"Westerners"* was, both then and later, a current euphemistic designation of the dead. In the west they dwelt *"honoured by the great god"*, that is by the king, surrounding him in the same hierarchy as during their lifetime. Part of the food and other supplies deemed necessary for their sustenance was deposited with them on the day of burial, but fresh supplies were brought now and then by relatives. The actual tomb and at least part of the equipment were expected to come from the king as a token of favour; they are the *hotp-di-nesu* "the satisfaction-which-the-king-gives".

Since there were too many applicants for such a favour, the gift in kind was very early replaced by a long list of these items introduced by the words *hotp-di-nesu* as a simple formula; but very early even this list was often summarized as *"thousand of bread and beer, oxen and fowl, alabaster (vessels) and clothing"*, where "thousand" stands for great numbers of each of these kinds of things. Various gods under whose protection the west stood in various localities were associated with the king as donors of this gift, and eventually the formula *hotp-di-nesu* meant hardly more than "prayer" addressed to these gods to bestow the tomb equipment and offerings in general upon the dead.

It was, however, only in part of Egypt, the narrow Nile valley proper, where the western desert is everywhere within sight and is never more than a few miles from the settlements situated along the river, that the west was the natural site for the world of the dead. In the north of the country, the Delta, where the western desert is too distant to be reached without a long journey, we find a different conception. The vast open horizons of the Delta seem to have been the original home of the idea that the world of the dead is in the sky, in which they have become stars. This conception was later blended with or superseded by the idea of a realm of the dead in the west, but clear traces of it come to light again and again.

During the Vth Dynasty, when the sun-religion of Heliopolis gained predominance, it was naturally the sky theory that was favoured, and the Pyramid texts offer vivid descriptions of how the dead king was imagined to reach heaven: now he ascended to it on a huge ladder, elsewhere he is said to have seized the tail of a heavenly cow, or again he flew up as a bird or was lifted up by the smoke of burning incense or by a sand storm. These details may be nothing more than the imagination of a poet, but they clearly show that the sky was the eventual abode of the dead.

The form which primitive imagination attributed to the supernatural and imperishable part of man, the soul, also points in the same direction. The soul left the body at the moment of death and flew away in the form of a bird. The bird was either *bai*, jabiru (*Mycteria ephippiorhynchus*, which is no longer found in Egypt) or *ikh*, crested ibis (*Ibis comata*), though the soul was able *"to take any form it liked"*. In the historical period *bai* and *ikh* were used, along with *ka* which will be dealt with presently, to designate the spiritual constituent of an individual, but it is impossible to define their nature exactly, nor was their precise nature quite clear to the Egyptians themselves. *Bai* eventually designates any form (not only that of a bird) which the soul may choose to take and Egyptologists translate it, therefore, either "external manifestation" or simply "soul"; the plural of the word, *bēw*, is the total of such manifestations which an individual is able to adopt and thus means "abilities", "power". *Ikh* is conveniently translated "spirit" or "shining spirit". "Shining" is the original meaning of the word applied to the bird because of the dazzling colouring of its feathers. The *bai*-bird has at all times remained a favourite symbol of the soul and was often even represented with a human head,

F

but by the time of the Middle Kingdom the transformation into an *ikh*-bird is no longer met with; the word was tending more and more to assume the meaning of a demon or ghost, and it is with this latter meaning alone that it survived in Coptic.

It is equally if not more difficult to explain to a modern mind the meaning conveyed by the notion of *ka*, the third spiritual part of man. It seems best, therefore, to quote the results arrived at by Sir Alan Gardiner after a thorough investigation of the subject: "The term appears to embrace the entire 'self' of a person regarded as an entity to some extent separable from that person. Modern concepts to which that of the *ka* occasionally corresponds are 'personality', 'soul', 'individuality', 'temperament'; the word may even mean a man's 'fortune' or 'position'. The Egyptians conceived of such notions in a more personal and tangible way than we do."

The Pyramid texts of the Vth and VIth Dynasties picture principally the fate of the king after death, but much of it was no doubt believed of the fate of any mortal. Their souls reached the sky, the goddess Nut, and as stars could be seen by night on her body. Nut was the *"one with a thousand souls"* (*kha-bēwes*); certainly all the numberless stars did not belong to dead kings, but included other humans as well. Under the influence of this belief the burial chamber of the tomb and the coffin, which were originally no more than the house of the deceased, were gradually transformed into a miniature image of the universe: the ceiling of the burial chamber is entirely decorated with rows of stars, and the lid of the coffin bears on its underside the figure of the goddess Nut, while the inscription on the coffin contains the welcoming words which Nut addressed to the deceased, her son, as well as the words of the earth-god Geb, whose son the deceased is also. Thus the king is aptly son of sky and earth, according to whether his spiritual (soul) or material (body) parts are envisaged.

In subsequent periods these conceptions, together with the use of the Pyramid texts, are extended from the king to all his subjects. But meanwhile the king had become the son of the sun-god Rē, and after death he joined his father in heaven to accompany him in his boat on his daily journey across the sky. It is quite natural that the common folk who, though never calling themselves sons of Rē, believed themselves to be Rē's creations, soon adopted the fate of the king.

What was it in the sun-religion that appealed so strangely to the Egyptian? It was partly that he saw the supreme importance of the sun, with its light and warmth, to the life of man and the whole of nature; Egyptians were aware that the sun was necessary to life and that without the sun there would be no earthly life. But this observation of a fact can hardly explain the final predominance of the solar religion. The cause of its victory lies rather in the supposed parallel which the Egyptian believed to exist between the life of the sun and that of man; and to the benefit and pleasure which he derived from the existence and daily course of the sun he added considerable comfort respecting his own existence after death.

The sun rises in the morning, shines all day and disappears in the evening on the western horizon. But this disappearance is only apparent and temporary, for the sun has not ceased to "live", the best proof being that it reappears the next morning after having spent the night in an invisible world. The Egyptians formed the conviction that human life is a close parallel to the course of the sun: man is born like the sun in the morning, lives his earthly life and dies, like the sun, which emits its life-giving rays the whole day and sets in the evening; but the analogy requires that his death should not be final, and that in a certain sense it does not take place at all. Man continues to live after the so-called death in a world outside his perception, and as a logical corollary, will at some time be born again to a new life. Thus the West, where both sun and men disappear, is called ōnkh "life"; both sun and men go there in order to "have a rest in life". Expressions like wahm ōnkh "who reiterates life" or, in late times, ankh hōtep "who lives and rests", are appended to the name of the deceased. The coffin, too, is called neb ōnkh "lord of life". The question as to when exactly and under what conditions the new or renewed life will take place is left undecided by the sun-religion, but these details did not matter very much. The deceased—like the king—took part in the nightly course of the sun as a spectator in the company of the sun-god. From the analogy between the sun and man, however, only a small step was needed to a complete identification of the two, where man, after physical death, was supposed to form part of the sun-god's substance, becoming "excellent spirit of Rē" (*ikh ōker en Rē*).

There were two other regularly recurring events, besides the course of the sun, which invited the sense of analogy innate in Egyptians to draw conclusions as to life, on the one hand, and death and a resumption of life after death, on the other. These two events were the overflowing of the Nile, the yearly rise of the river, and, following it, a luxuriant springing into life of all vegetation which had previously been brought to a standstill and almost annihilated by the excessive heat. This life-bringing moisture from the Nile and the renewal of vegetable life could not fail to impress profoundly an agricultural people and were very early connected with the person of the god Osiris.

Two diametrically opposed opinions have been formed among Egyptologists as to the origin of the personality of this god. According to one theory Osiris was originally a human king who in the very remote past reigned over the whole land of Egypt from his capital in the eastern Delta. His violent death through drowning, caused by his brother, the god Sētekh, is interpreted as the death of a king in a rebellion led by the town of Ombos in Upper Egypt, seat of the worship of the god Sētekh; this resulted in the division of the country into two separate Kingdoms, the North and the South, which were later united again after a victorious campaign by the North. This victory and the re-establishment of the original kingdom would then be reflected in the myth by the victory of Osiris' son, the god Horus, over Sētekh. The dead Osiris, however, was deified and a personal creed was attached to his life and death, which was very much like that of Christianity based on the suffering and death of Jesus.

The creed assigned the rule over the dead to a risen Osiris, and saw in this and in the eventual defeat of Sētekh a symbol of the victory of the principle of good and justice over evil. The goddess Isis, sister and wife of Osiris, is, by this theory, only a personification of Osiris' throne, since the name Isis (Egn. *Eset*) really means "seat", and the other sister, the goddess Nephthys (Egn. *Nebthut*), is a personification of Osiris' residence, also in accordance with the meaning of her name "lady of a castle".

But whereas this theory interprets the myth of Osiris as a memory of historical events, the rival theory sees in Osiris a personification of the overflowing of the Nile and of the rebirth of vegetable life which follows the floods. Such a conception of Osiris as god of vegetation was current in Egypt in all periods of her later history, and may have existed at the very moment when his name is first met with in written records. But in the few passages in the texts of the pyramid of Unis which have been quoted to prove the original nature of Osiris as the god of the Nile floods, it is not Osiris who is identified, or rather compared, with the Nile flood, but the dead king Unis. "*It is Unis who inundates the land and who has come forth from the lake, it is Unis who plucks the papyrus-plant,*" says Pyr. 388, and similarly Pyr. 507–508, "*Unis came today from the fullness of the flood, he is Sūbek, with a green feather, watchful face and uplifted fore-part of the body . . . he came to his pools which are on the shore inundated by the Great Fullness, to the place of satisfaction, with green fields (the place) which is in the realm of light. Unis has appeared as Subek, son of Neith.*" The reason for the king's connexion with the floods in the second passage is merely that he is compared with the crocodile (god Sūbek) emerging from the water and lurking for prey and food. It is only because complete identification of King Unis with Osiris was assumed throughout this oldest version of the Pyramid texts that the two passages could be adduced to prove that Osiris was a personification of natural phenomena.

This identity, however, exists only in one part of the texts, namely those relating to the ceremony of presenting the offerings, where the beneficiary is invariably addressed as "Osiris Unis". This is, therefore, a contemporary adaptation, while everywhere else in the older parts of the texts the dead king is not identical with Osiris; on the contrary, more than once he is this god's son Horus. But he comes to occupy the throne of Osiris and to rule like him, and Osiris is requested to announce his arrival to the gods. Thus the dead king is a repetition of Osiris, his case is analogous to that of Osiris, or the king endeavours to imitate him. The aspect of Osiris as a ruler of the spirits of the dead (*ikh*) is quite prominent, but no other feature of his character is noticeable. The inscriptions in the pyramid of Unis cannot, therefore, be adduced to prove Osiris to be the god of the Nile floods from the very outset.

In the later versions of Pyramid texts this state of things changes, and Osiris is connected with the flooding of the Nile on several occasions; but in view of the absence of this trait in the oldest text, it would rather seem that Osiris received this character from the king of the living, whose poetical identification with inundation and vegetation was probably the last relic of the primitive belief that in addition to ruling over his subjects, a chief also had command of these natural phenomena. This identification with Osiris was at first the prerogative of the king; later it was extended to other members of the royal family, and the pyramids of the queens display pyramid texts with this identification at the end of the VIth Dynasty. Finally, by laying more stress on the aspect of death than on that of kingship, this identification was extended to any private individual; the character of Osiris passed from deified kingship and its resurrection after death to a semblance of its former state, to the resurrection after death of life in general. This also included the whole of nature, especially its two recurrent phenomena, the inundation and the growth of vegetation. Osiris became the symbol of personality and life persisting through death.

Nothing was more natural for the Egyptian mind than to imagine a parallel between resurrection and a growing seed; in a text originating during the First Intermediate Period the soul of the dead is compared with Napri, the personification of corn, *"who lives after he has died"*. From the Middle Kingdom onwards, Osiris is often referred to as the god of floods and vegetation, and in the New Kingdom his character as the symbol of vegetable life is well demonstrated by the occurrence in tombs of the "Corn-Osiris". This consists of a wooden box in the shape of the mummified Osiris; the box was filled with earth in which corn seeds were planted. The earth was watered and the corn brought to germination so that the young plants shot up through holes in the lid of the box. In another case the earth in the shape of Osiris was heaped up on linen fabric stretched over a reed mat in a wooden frame.

Having become the prototype of all the departed, Osiris and his cult spread irresistibly through the country. After initial hostility he was adopted by the Solar religion and incorporated in the Ennead of gods of Heliopolis as the son of the earth-god Geb. His worship was carried on and propagated by his devotees rather than by the temples and the hierarchy of priests, though both of these existed. Osiris gradually absorbed the local funerary deities and found a permanent centre for his cult at Abydos, probably at the time when he was still chiefly the deified conception of dead kingship, for the tombs of the earliest Pharaohs were situated at Abydos. The tomb of one of these kings, King Djer of the Ist Dynasty, was identified with the tomb of Osiris and a temple of Osiris was built in the town of Abydos itself. The town became a place of pilgrimage where Egyptians from all parts of the country were either actually buried, or built cenotaphs or at least set up stelae at the "*staircase*" of Osiris. King Sethos I of the XIXth Dynasty built a fine funerary temple at Abydos which had a subterranean cenotaph, though he already had a temple and a rock-tomb at Thebes.

Keeping in mind the characteristic conservatism of the Egyptian mind, which was unable to discard old ideas when new conceptions appeared, we are not surprised that the identification of the dead with Osiris did not mean parting with the ancient spells which were recited during the funerary ceremonies and whose aim was to safeguard the existence and welfare of the deceased by magic. On the contrary, a great many of the spells known from the Pyramid texts were taken over for the use of the common people and new ones of both the same and similar kinds were added to this old stock. But they were not only recited during funerals; it was thought useful that they should be within the reach of the deceased at any moment when he might be in need of them, and so they were first set forth on the walls of coffins—we then call them Coffin Texts—and from the Middle Kingdom they were written on papyrus and deposited with the body of the deceased. This latter stage is the so-called "Book of the Dead", and it should always be remembered that this is not a systematic treatise on the Egyptian beliefs regarding life after death, still less on Egyptian religion, as has often been intimated in popular accounts of Egyptian religion, but a haphazard collection of magical practices. The Egyptians themselves were well aware of this rather primitive character of the Book of the Dead and attempts were not lacking to mitigate its crudeness by symbolic interpretation, a common line of development in all religions.

Among the various kinds of help which these spells (or chapters) afford to the dead are protection against hunger and thirst in the Beyond, the power of assuming various animal forms, and especially the "coming-forth at daytime" (*pīret-em-hrow*), that is, emerging into the light from the darkness of the tomb to partake of the funerary offerings. This was so important that the expression *pīret-em-hrow* became the Egyptian title for the whole Book of the Dead.

In the Pyramid texts the possession and knowledge of magic spells is an all-important means of attaining power and happiness after death. This is perhaps natural, since these texts were originally designed for the king who, being himself a god, stood above mortals. For private individuals a more refined conception grew up, gradually competing with the mere reliance on the power of magic: happiness in the Beyond is a reward for and conditioned by virtuous and righteous behaviour in earthly life.

In this respect the Egyptians desired to resemble Osiris, who had been indicted by Sētekh before Rē and his circle of gods in Heliopolis, but with the help of Thoth had been declared by these divine judges to be "true of voice" (*ma-khrow*), that is justified or innocent. Aspiring towards resurrection and life after death like Osiris and at identification with him, man also had to receive the divine verdict, this time from Osiris himself, who was now the ruler of the dead. This verdict was a result of "*computes*" of a man's actions, and the scene of judgment is the subject of the well-known illustration frequently accompanying the 125th chapter of the Book of the Dead.

The judgment takes place before Osiris and his forty-two

assessors. The corresponding chapter or spell 125 consists of two sets (originally there were clearly two separate versions of this chapter) of denials by the deceased of evil actions and qualities, each negative statement of the second set being addressed to one of the assessors of Osiris. The scene depicted, however, takes no notice of these denials by the deceased, who is represented as being led by the hand before the judges by Horus. In front of Osiris a balance is set up attended by the god Anubis, while the wise Thoth calculates on his scribe's palette the result of the weighing of the dead man's heart against Truth.

On the scales the heart is weighed against Truth, which is represented either by its symbol, an ostrich feather, or by a seated statuette of the goddess of Truth, Ma'et, with an ostrich feather on her head. In the illustrations the two scales of the balance are always represented in perfect equilibrium which is evidently the ideal to be aimed at, favourable to the dead, where the weight of the heart, the seat of the will and instigator of man's actions, was exactly equal to that of truth. It is not known what the weight of the heart of a sinner was supposed to be, whether evil actions made the heart too heavy, or whether the lack of good actions made it lighter than Truth; it is only certain that there was a difference in weight between Truth and a sinful heart.

If the result of the weighing was satisfactory the deceased was declared to be *"true of voice"* like Osiris and entitled to life and happiness in his kingdom; but if the test was unsatisfactory, the deceased was destroyed by the *"devourer of the dead"*, a monster waiting by the side of the balance, a mixture of crocodile, lion and hippopotamus.

In view of this assessment of the moral value of the deceased, it is difficult to see in the text of this chapter of the Book of the Dead (often called with a considerable degree of exaggeration the "Negative Confession") more than another magic spell, a relapse into the more primitive trend of thought where a clear conscience could be assured by mere words. But the denial of sins contained in this spell is itself a proof of the acceptance of a moral standard as the most important factor in attaining life and happiness in the future life. This ethical movement makes its appearance with the Osirian belief and henceforward Osiris is always closely connected with it.

The preservation of the dead body was another condition for survival after death which only gradually gained in importance. Corpses of the prehistoric period show no attempt at artificial preservation, but isolated cases of mummification have been observed as early as the first dynasties. In the IVth Dynasty mummification was no longer rare, as is shown by the existence of contemporary canopic jars, which are closely connected with mummification. These are four vessels in which the viscera extracted from the dead body were preserved; each jar was under the protection of one of the four sons of Horus, whose names were Imset, Hapy, Duamūtef, and Kebehsenuf. Fear of the complete destruction of the body led to the development of an elaborate method of embalming, and a great effort was made to preserve the physical features of the body and, in so doing, the identity of the deceased.

In the IVth Dynasty a temporary custom appears to counteract the possible loss of the most important part of the body, the head, by burying in the tomb a "substitute head" in stone carefully portraying the facial traits. The dry climate of the country helped greatly in the natural desiccation of the bodies and thus in their preservation, and probably this natural process is at the root of the belief that preservation of the body is a thing to be striven for and almost a condition for the survival of personality.

The care for the preservation of the body is also shown by the change from the use of wooden coffins to stone ones, and by increasing their number to two or three for the same body, or in the case of royal burials to an even greater number.

These ideas concerning life after death sufficiently explain the presence in the tombs of various kinds of equipment, especially objects of daily use. It remains for us to touch upon a few others, the origin of which is less obvious and which are too frequently found and too characteristic of ancient Egypt to be passed over in silence.

Chapter 30 of the Book of the Dead is another instance of getting round the ethical requirement of sinlessness in the judgment of the dead by a magical incantation; this chapter is addressed to the heart, which the Egyptian held to be the most important factor whose favour had to be sought. This he did with the following words: *"O my heart of my mother, O my heart of my mother! O my breast of my (various) forms, O my breast of my forms! Stand not forth against me as witness, combat me not in the assembly (of judges), be not hostile to me before the Keeper of the Balance. Thou art my ka that is in my body, the Khnum who makes my limbs prosperous. Go forth towards happiness, let us hasten there. Make not my name to stink with the nobles who make men into heaps (?). (So it will be) best for us, and best for the Hearer (of pleas), and joy to the verdict-giver. Plan no lies against me in the presence of the great god; behold, that which thou discernest is!"* From the end of the Second Intermediate Period this spell is found carved on the flat bases of large stone amulets the upper part of which is cut in the form of a scarab, the Egyptian dung-beetle. The scarab has always been the symbol of the birth of the sun and of the birth of life in general; covered with Chapter 30 of the Book of the Dead it served as a substitute for the heart of the dead and was, therefore, placed on the chest of the mummy on top of its wrappings. The close connexion of these scarabs ("heart scarabs") with the heart is also sometimes indicated by cutting the outline of their bases in the shape of a heart.

The views of the Egyptians on the nature of the life beyond, in the *"other land"* as they called it sometimes to distinguish it from *"this land"*, were subject to changes despite their stubborn conservatism. And thus the relatively simple original views concerning life after death became rather blurred and confused with time. Until the middle of the XVIIIth Dynasty the prevalent opinion was that life after death was a simple replica of earthly existence. This is evident not only from objects found in tombs, but especially from the paintings and sculptures in the tombs of those who could afford such decoration. There the deceased is shown surrounded by his family, friends and subordinates, as well as by his possessions, or accompanying his chief or his king, pursuing his occupations and entertainments, in short in full enjoyment of all the wealth which he has attained.

There has been a controversy among Egyptologists as to

the purpose of these scenes: some were convinced that the paintings and reliefs, which represented all that the deceased had attained in his earthly life, were supposed to become new realities in the life beyond by magical potency which we know the Egyptians attributed to pictures of things, as well as to the spoken and written word. Some again denied this purpose and attributed the occurrence of the paintings and reliefs exclusively to the pride of the tomb-owners and to the artistic urge which is an outstanding feature of the Egyptian people. Though both these two factors certainly contributed to the rise of the custom, the "magical explanation" seems to prevail at present for the bulk of the tomb decoration. Expressions like *"eternally"*, which now and then accompany the pictures, can best be explained by assuming that the pictures were intended to preserve or renew the reality of the scene. Moreover, relatively little room is given to individual events in the past life of the deceased, in biographies for instance, on which to base our suspicions that boastfulness was the chief or only reason. Sometimes, indeed, the pictures and reliefs occur in rooms which were not intended to be accessible to the public after the burial, or again the pictures are restricted to funerary rites where the perpetuation after death was certainly the only preoccupation of the tomb owner.

Towards the end of the Old Kingdom, and especially during the First Intermediate Period and the Middle Kingdom, the reliefs and pictures on the tomb walls were often replaced by small wooden figures of the servants or craftsmen of the deceased, his buildings, garden, cattle or ships. These figures were grouped on wooden planks so as to form whole scenes of the same nature as those represented elsewhere in pictures on the walls of the tomb; besides ships with their equipment and full crews, we find the registration by scribes of corn carried in sacks by servants into granaries, the reviewing of cattle, scenes of spinning, weaving, carpentry, butchery, brewing beer, baking, etc. These models too, often of an exquisite workmanship, are mostly deposited in the inaccessible room containing the coffin with the body of the deceased and are, therefore, clearly the substitutes for his earthly property which are to accompany him into the life beyond.

Until well on in the Middle Kingdom, therefore, the prevalent belief was that menial work was done for a wealthy man in the life beyond and that this work was performed by servants represented either in pictures on the walls of the tomb or in the form of statuettes buried in his funeral chamber. It is not certain what ideas the working classes held about their future life; but it can be conjectured that they found it quite natural that they should continue working for their lord in the house or in the fields in the life beyond. Names were often added to the pictures of servants in a hasty scratch, contrasting with the carefully executed official inscriptions of the tomb, or were jotted down in ink on their wooden statuettes, a proof that not just any servants were supposed to accompany the deceased, but the very individuals who served him during his life-time; it is even likely that by identifying themselves with the persons represented in pictures or sculpture the servants sought for a guarantee of an existence after death.

It was probably during the social upheaval of the First Intermediate Period that a different conception was formed which made menial labour obligatory to any dead person, irrespective of the station which he or she had held in earthly life. At the same time a magic spell, later incorporated as Chapter 6 of the Book of the Dead, was composed to avoid the labour in the fields of the other world. Small models of the mummy of the dead in small coffins begin to appear in the tombs, and the spell in question was evidently intended to summon these to impersonate the dead at the morning roll-call for work in the fields. The spell with its title runs as follows:

"*Spell to cause the shawabti to perform work for a man in the Netherworld: O shawabti, if So and So is called upon or if I am listed to perform any work that is performed in the Netherworld as a man to carry out his duties, to cultivate the fields, to water the banks (of the river), to transport the sand of the East to the West, 'Present', so shalt thou say.*"

Gradually the imitations of the mummy are replaced by small figures of the living, usually of baked clay, less often of stone or wood, and very occasionally of metal. In the arms crossed on the chest they carry the characteristic tools for work in the fields, a hoe and a sack. These figures are often inscribed with Chapter 6 of the Book of the Dead which also reveals their Egyptian name *shawabti*, which later became *ushebti*. The original meaning of the word is not known with certainty; possibly it is connected with the name of the persea-tree (*shawab*), but in the New Kingdom the current form *ushebti* was interpreted as "answerer" to fit their function of answering the roll-call instead of the dead.

When at the end of the Middle Kingdom the custom of burying statuettes of servants in the tombs disappeared, the function of the servant-figures was transferred to the *ushebti* which now assumed the double role of the impersonation of the dead and of his servants. Correspondingly there is no longer only one *ushebti* for a dead person, but several; their number steadily grows, and in later times there are even as many as 365, one for every day of the year, and *ushebtis* of overseers are added for every ten *ushebtis* of working type.

The custom of depositing food and other necessaries with the dead for their use in a future life, which originated in primitive conceptions about life after death, was never completely abandoned, though later this funerary equipment was sometimes only symbolically indicated. Thus small stone models of various pieces of meat replaced actual food; garments, sandals, jewels, etc., are painted inside the coffins of the First Intermediate Period and of the Middle Kingdom. During the latter period various objects occur, such as crowns and sceptres, the presence of which can only be explained by assuming that the custom originated with kings and was only later extended to persons of non-royal blood, the same process being true of the funerary texts written on the coffins of the same period. Later in the New Kingdom many of these objects are found again as amulets made of stone, faience or metal and disposed all over the mummified body.

We have seen how manifold and conflicting were the ideas about the fate of human beings after death. They ascended to the sky to continue their existence there as stars, or they continued their earthly life enjoying all they had attained; or again they were subjected to hard agricultural work, joined Osiris to take part in his rule of the Underworld, or joined the sun-god Rē in his barque to accompany him on his journey across the sky during the day and in the subterranean world at night.

This night journey of the sun-god is the subject of two books, the "Book of Gates" and the "Book of him who is in the Underworld" (so-called *Amduat*, more correctly *Amdē*). These are another two examples of that curious funerary literature which the Egyptians alone among the peoples of all times and lands deposited with their dead. Originally these two books hardly represented any current beliefs about the world beyond except for the basic idea of the nocturnal voyage of the sun. They are fantastic creations of pseudo-learned brains, but cannot be passed over in silence because they form the contents of the majority of the texts and representations covering walls of both tombs and sarcophagi of the kings of the New Kingdom in the Valley of the Kings from Tuthmosis I onwards. Later, however, under the XXIst Dynasty, these texts also appear on papyrus in a much abbreviated form in the graves of people of non-royal descent. It is impossible to convey an idea of the contents of these two formidable literary compositions in a few lines. The texts appear to be of secondary importance to the illustrations in these two works.

The "Book of him who is in the Underworld" makes no reference to the dead at all, and Osiris is seldom mentioned; it only describes the night journey of the sun-god through the dark realm of the other world from west to east. This world is divided into twelve regions, each corresponding to one of the twelve hours of the night, and each is in the charge of some god and is populated by other gods, as well as good and bad demons of uncouth appearance and peculiar names. The idea of the "Book of Gates" is similar: it describes the journey of the sun at night, through an Underworld divided into compartments each of which is entered through a fortified gate. Each gate is watched by a guardian armed with a knife.

As there were good and bad people among the living, so there were also good and bad among the dead. The spirits of the latter were to be feared; they tried to do harm to the living, especially to children, and protection against them was sought by means of incantations and talismans. The deceased members of a family were helpful even after death if appropriate care was taken of their tombs and offerings. It was possible to communicate with them by means of letters written on papyrus or linen, or by messages written on the dishes in which food was brought to the dead. Thus the dead were supposed to continue to show interest in the affairs of the living and were powerful enough to help them in their difficulties.

Apart from the worship of parents there was no widespread cult of more remote ancestors, though cases are known where individuals attended the tombs of their ancestors for several generations back. As will be seen in the next chapter, the tomb was the proper place for the worship of the dead, but in New Kingdom villages nameless busts were found in small niches in the walls inside the houses, and it is thought that these represented the deceased near relatives of the family, who were worshipped in the homes where they had lived.

CHAPTER IV

THE CULT

MAN expresses his religious feelings by repeating a series of actions, which constitute a form of worship or cult. These actions are arranged in a certain order, ceremony or rite, and follow an underlying idea.

The Egyptian mind was consistent in regarding the living, the gods and the dead as, to use Sir Alan Gardiner's words, "three species of the same genus *anthropos*, all three subject to the same physical needs, to the same habits and desires". These could best be observed in the living, whose requirements were food and drink, water for washing, perfumes and clothes, but also a house, rest and recreation. The Egyptians logically assumed that all these needs were shared by the gods and the dead, if they were to continue their existence, and the purpose of the divine and funerary cult was to ensure that the needs were satisfied.

In very early times the dwellings of all three, the house of the living, the temple of the god and the tomb of the dead, were constructed on very much the same pattern. The higher position occupied by the gods and the dead, is, however, shown by the fact that while an ordinary human being lived in a house and only a king had a "palace", the temple was called "god's castle" and the tomb "castle of the *ka*". Another important difference was that, whereas the earthly house, including the king's palace, was built of some perishable material, sun-baked bricks, reeds or wood, the permanence of both the temple and the tomb was assured by employing stone for their construction or by carving them in the living rock.

The changes through which the plan of the house and, after a short lapse of time, that of the tomb passed towards the close of the prehistoric period are exactly parallel. The original circular hut became first rectangular with rounded corners and finally a perfect rectangle. The subterranean part of the grave

97

G

follows the same course. Owing to a complete disappearance of all early sanctuaries a parallel development cannot be shown in the case of the temple, but it is significant that later representations of the primitive sanctuary of Min, who is the earliest god safely attested, depict a conical hut, clearly rounded and not unlike the pointed huts still found with many African tribes.

All three types of building contained rooms in which the owner—the living, the god or the dead—lived and parts where his possessions were kept. Servants provided for the comfort of the living, priests (lit. "god's servants") for that of the god and special funerary priests, called "servants of the *ka*", cared for the needs of the dead.

The presence of vessels containing food and drink in prehistoric tombs shows that these two elements were thought essential for the existence and welfare of the dead, and the oldest written evidence which we possess confirms that the meal formed also the most important part of the daily funerary rite. The same is true of offerings regularly presented to the gods.

A funerary or temple ceremony began with the pouring of water over the officiant's hands and the burning of incense. In these two acts the officiant represented the beneficiary himself; they were the preliminaries to every Egyptian repast. Then the dead or the god was presented with unguents and napkins and finally censed. A libation of water which followed represented the practice of the washing of the mouth customary before each meal. Only when this prelude was finished was the food brought in.

There were undoubtedly other ceremonies which varied with the locality and with the character attributed to different deities, but very little record of these has come down to us owing to an early and all-pervading desire for uniformity. About the time of the IIIrd Dynasty the worship of the Heliopolitan sun-god Rē-Atum began to gain ground and from the IVth Dynasty onward, under the influence of the sun-cult, we have clear proof of the acceptance of the belief that the Egyptian king, who had previously been regarded as an embodiment of the god Horus, was also considered to be a son of the sun-god Rē or even the sun-god himself. For the sake of their religious and political prestige a number of the greater gods had to allow themselves to become identified with or assimilated to Rē, and the result was that their daily temple ritual was in course of time permeated with elements derived from the solar ritual of Heliopolis. Minor deities who preserved their original individual character followed suit. With that conservatism so characteristic of the ancient Egyptians, the special feature of the older daily ritual, namely the banquet, was not given up, but was incorporated in the new Heliopolitan rite. By the end of the Old Kingdom the daily liturgy in the temples of all gods and goddesses throughout the land was the same.

According to the Heliopolitan belief the sun-god emerged, in the first instance, from the primaeval ocean Nun, and was reborn each morning when the sun reappeared in the sky after washing in the Fields of Iaru or in the Fields of Life. Another belief interpreted this reappearance as the rebirth of an infant god from the womb of the sky-goddess Nut. The king, in his capacities as the sun-god's son, the sun-god himself and the chief priest, had, therefore, to undergo a similar daily purification before being dressed and equipped with the royal insignia. Consequently purification, or the libation substituted for it, became a vital element in any liturgy, and bodily purity and cleanliness were required of the king, the priest and the layman, as well as of the god and the dead. Water became the medium of rebirth and life-giving qualities were attributed to it. Every temple was provided with a sacred pool for the purpose of purification and libation. The matutinal rite, which opened with the ceremony of purification, caused the verb "to rise in the morning" to acquire a general meaning of "praising" or "praying".

Ritual practices, already rather involved, became still further complicated when the myth and worship of Osiris spread from their original home at Busiris in the Delta to the rest of Egypt. This process, like the development of the sun-cult, was completed by the end of the Vth Dynasty and the rites then existing had to take into account the dead king and the god Osiris. The son of Osiris was Horus, but Horus was also the living king and chief priest, consequently his father, the dead king, became Osiris.

There were several forms of the myth telling how the dead

Osiris was brought to life by his son Horus. According to one of the two traditions most generally accepted, Horus gave Osiris his eye to eat and so brought him back to life. The other version was influenced by the Heliopolitan rite of lustration: according to this version the dead Osiris was washed by the gods Horus and Thoth and this washing brought his corpse to life again, but he was not reborn with a new body like the sun-god Rē.

The Osirianization of the temple liturgy did not change its form, which remained solar and Heliopolitan, but new interpretations were added to it. Thus the sun-god, who was formerly believed to have been washed every day by the goddess of the cool water Kebhowet, was now supposed to be washed by the gods Horus and Thoth, the lustrators of Osiris. But the Egyptians went even further. They did not discard the resurrection of Osiris through eating the eye of Horus, but identified each item of the divine and funerary repast with the eye of Horus.

The body of Osiris had been dismembered after death by his enemies and now when the dead human king was identified with Osiris, the corpse of the king was also represented as dismembered. And as Osiris's members had been revived by washing, the body of the dead king was also supposed to be joined together again by a lustral washing. This occurred during the embalmment and the embalmers played in it the role of the gods Horus and Thoth, probably wearing their masks. The water used for this washing was identified with the vital fluid or sweat which had emanated from the body of Osiris. Since the mysterious sources of the Nile had from time immemorial been located at Elephantine, that is the First Cataract, the lustration water was said to come from there. Consequently the tomb which concealed the body of Osiris, or at least a part of it, was placed in that region. In this way Osiris was identified with the Nile and its floods.

After the end of the Old Kingdom a vast wave of democratization passed through Egyptian religious and funerary ideas and conceptions, and all those privileges which had formerly been the prerogatives of the king were now transferred to other mortals: every dead person was now identified with Osiris, and his son or any officiant performing the rites in his stead was regarded as Horus.

After these preliminaries, which were necessary to explain even the main elements of the remarkably complex notions underlying Egyptian ritual, we shall proceed to describe the various rites which—let it be pointed out again—all had as their basis the original liturgical repast combined with the Heliopolitan lustration or libation.

The daily temple liturgy is preserved in two versions. One consists of a series of reliefs and accompanying texts in several chapels of the temple of Osiris at Abydos; the other, dating from the XXIInd Dynasty, relates to Amun and is found in a hieratic papyrus in the Berlin Museum. Both versions are, however, essentially identical and together give the following picture of the ceremony:

Before entering the temple the priest had to purify himself in the sacred pool. On his arrival at the temple he first kindled a fire and filled a censer with burning charcoal and incense. He then proceeded towards the shrine in which the god had spent the night. He broke the clay seal on the door, pushed away the bolts, and opened the two wings of the door. The statue of the god appeared to him and the priest saluted the god, casting himself upon the ground before the statue. He then chanted one or more hymns and offered honey to the god, burning more incense while making four circumambulations around the statue. Alternatively, he offered the deity a figure of Ma'et, the goddess of Truth. Finally, he took the statue out of its shrine, removed the old clothing and anointed it with unguent.

The actual toilet began after he had placed the statue on a little pile of sand spread on the ground, perhaps to represent the desert from behind which the sun appeared every morning. He again censed the deity and sprinkled it with water out of four *namset*-vessels and four red vessels. After repeating the censing he cleansed the statue's mouth with three different kinds of natron and dressed it with the head-cloth and garments of various colours, replaced its jewels, anointed it and painted its eyelids with green and black eye-paints. Finally, he invested the god with the royal insignia.

Then followed a repast. The priest put the god back in its

shrine, purified the altar and then laid the food and drink before the god. He raised each course separately, offering it to the god. The banquet finished, he closed the door of the shrine and sealed it. He purified the room removing his footprints with special care and left the room. At every stage in the ceremony the priest recited appropriate words or formulae.

The lustration which the king underwent before officiating as high-priest of a god was of a similar kind. It was performed in a special annexe of the temple called the "House of the Morning" because the lustration took place at dawn. The king was sprinkled with water from the sacred pool by two priests impersonating either Horus and Thoth or Horus and Sētekh and perhaps wearing the masks of these gods during the ceremony. The lustration, accompanied by the recital of appropriate formulae, imbued the king with "life and good fortune" and renewed his youth. After the purification with water the king was fumigated with incense and four balls of natron were served to him to chew. In subsequent ceremonies the king was successively dressed, anointed and equipped with ornaments and the insignia of his kingly power. He was then ready to enter the temple and officiate as the priest of the god according to the daily temple liturgy which has already been described.

The ceremony of purification undergone by the living king was also performed on the body of the dead king and indeed on the bodies of all deceased persons to make them pure as the sun-god and Osiris, who, after his death, had himself been asperged by certain divinities in this way. Such a lustration was possible only before the body was buried, that is during the embalmment and at the funeral. But as the sun-god was believed to undergo the lustration and to be reborn every morning, means were devised to repeat the lustration and the repast connected with it on behalf of the dead during the daily funeral liturgy. The corpse itself being inaccessible, lying in the burial-chamber at the bottom of the tomb-shaft, the lustration was replaced by a libation offered in the chapel of the pyramid-temple (or later a funerary temple) in the case of a king, and in the cult-chamber of the tomb superstructure in the case of a private person. For this purpose a more durable and lifelike substitute for the dead body was made, namely a statue. In the presence of this statue the libation was made and the offering of food and drink presented. We have already seen that in the temple the liturgical rites on behalf of a god were also performed before a statue, a visible and tangible image of the god.

But before a statue was assigned to this purpose, a ceremony called the "Opening of the Mouth" was performed on it in the sculptor's workshop (called "Castle of the Gold"). By this ceremony the statue was identified with the god or with a human being and endowed with his life and power.

The ceremony of the "Opening of the Mouth" consisted of a number of peculiar rites. It was ancient in origin, the first mention of it occurring as early as the beginning of the IVth Dynasty. The earliest complete account of it dates, however, from the XIXth Dynasty, when it was embodied in a long ceremony performed at funerals in or before the tomb; in that instance the rites were performed upon the mummy and not a statue. The body of the deceased person was thus given life and his faculties were renewed so that he might benefit from the daily funerary service to be conducted in the chapel of his tomb.

In this expanded version the rite consisted of many acts, among which the "Opening of the Mouth" proper occupied the central position. It was preceded and followed by two rites already known from the daily temple liturgy; in fact the Heliopolitan washing and dressing ceremonies, followed by the repast, formed the basis of these two rites.

The first part corresponded with the lustration ceremony: the statue was placed on the sand with its face to the south, it was purified with water, balls of natron were presented to purify its mouth, and again it was fumigated with incense. After the performance of these rites there followed a rather obscure conversation strongly influenced by the Osiris myth, between the priests entering the workshop and the sculptors. Then an ox was slaughtered, its foreleg cut off and the heart taken out, after which a goat and a goose were beheaded. The foreleg and the heart were presented to the statue, its mouth touched with the foreleg and various tools (adzes and chisels) and water was offered. These ceremonies were supposed to open the mouth and the eyes of the statue and to give it the faculties of a living person.

The third and last part of the whole ceremony was a repetition of the toilet enacted in other rites: a head-dress, clothes and jewels were placed on the statue; it was anointed and invested with royal insignia, and finally fumigated with incense. This was followed by a repast served on an altar or offering table which had first been purified. Finally, the statue was solemnly transported to its place.

An interesting feature of the repast in this ceremony was its composition, for the bull, two gazelles and a Nile-goose were relics of a more primitive meal. All three creatures were the quarry of the Egyptian at a time when he was predominantly a hunter, though as early as the Old Kingdom they had been domesticated and bred on farms.

There is no Egyptian account of the rites performed during mummification. We possess, however, two papyri, one at the Louvre, the other at Cairo, of the Ptolemaic period, dealing with the Ritual of Embalmment, but they are both incomplete and are chiefly concerned with formulae uttered by the priests officiating during various ceremonies and are extremely obscure owing to their numerous mythological allusions. Many actual mummies have, of course, been preserved and some of them examined; they show that the art of embalming developed gradually and varied at different periods. But even at a given period several degrees of mummification differing in price were practised and the poorer classes never seem to have been able to afford the expense involved; instead they relied simply on the natural desiccation of the body resulting from contact with the warm sand.

Embalmment was generally begun soon after death; but at some periods it was delayed till the corpse had begun to decay. The embalmers called at the house of the deceased, placed the body on a bier and took it to their workshop which was a tent called "the place of purification" or "the good house". The process of embalmment lasted in most cases seventy days. It was but an imitation of a treatment which the dead god Osiris was believed to have been the first to receive; the dead person, therefore, became Osiris through the embalmment of his corpse and the embalmers impersonated the gods who took part in the mummification of Osiris. The chief embalmer was the god Anubis, his assistants were identified with the sons of Horus and of Khentekhtay. The "sem"-priest and the lector-priest ("Khery-hebet") gave instructions to the embalmers and recited the appropriate spells.

The process of embalmment began with washing the body with Nile water; then the intestines (the parts most subject to decomposition), were removed, the body was soaked in salt (natron), and impregnated and covered with oils, unguents and resins; various amulets were then placed upon it, it was wrapped entirely in linen bandages and placed in a coffin. Washing with water was a solar purification and the water used for it was believed to be imbued with vital power. It was, therefore, carefully collected in jars, and these, together with other materials used for mummification as well as the wooden table on which the operations were performed, were buried in the vicinity of the tomb. An incision in the left flank enabled the viscera to be removed and replaced by balls of linen; the heart, however, was left in the body. The organs which had been taken out were preserved in four jars called by Egyptologists "Canopic". The brain was in most cases removed through the nostrils by means of a metal hook. In earlier periods linen models were substituted for soft external parts of the body; later mud and sand were packed under the skin to preserve the original form. The materials used for embalming included myrrh, cedar oil, incense, wax, honey, flax for making bandages, olive oil, etc.; all of these were believed to have exuded from the body of the gods or to have been created by the tears of the gods falling on the ground when they wept for the death of Osiris. They endued the dead with the power of these gods.

The burial ceremonies are also known to us only from representations on the walls of tombs, and, though they occur fairly frequently, many details are very obscure. Among these are two journeys made by the deceased, one to Busiris in Lower Egypt, the other to Abydos in Upper Egypt, during which a barque containing the dead is seen towed by one or more sailing ships. It seems that these journeys were only pictorial reminders of a king's burial. The king's body was transported to Busiris to appear there as the dead King Osiris accompanied by his Lower Egyptian subjects, and to Abydos to take part in the festivals of Osiris. When ordinary people adopted representations of a king's burial for their own use, the two scenes in question were retained, though they no longer corresponded with reality. They are probably also to some extent confused with the crossing of the Nile by the funeral procession when the cemetery lay on the opposite bank to the home of the deceased.

The body was carried to the tomb in a coffin placed on a boat in the middle of a long procession. The boat was dragged on a sledge by men and oxen while milk was poured on the road; male relatives and friends of the deceased followed. Two women impersonating Isis and Nephthys and called "kites" accompanied the coffin kneeling one at the head and one at the foot. It is quite possible, however, that sometimes they were not the widow and one of the female relatives, but only two statues placed on the boat. Another sledge with a box containing canopic jars with the viscera of the deceased followed the coffin. A group of other women, including professional female mourners, walked together all clad in grey-blue, the colour of mourning, crying loudly, shedding tears, tearing their garments, beating their bodies and pouring dust on their heads and clothes. Priests burning incense and reading funerary formulae walked in the procession. At the end followed a long line of servants carrying funerary equipment, such as furniture, vases and chests with clothes and jewels, to be deposited in the tomb.

Musicians and dancers waited at the tomb for the procession. On its arrival the ritual of "Opening of the Mouth" was performed on the mummy standing upright before the tomb, and the mummy was then lowered into the burial chamber. All the mourners were entertained to a banquet on returning from the funeral.

At nearly all periods the corpse was deposited underground. The superstructure of the tomb passed through many changes according to changing artistic skill and taste. Its origin seems to have been a tumulus, a low heap of sand or stones piled up on the ground above the place where the body was buried. This served a twofold purpose; it prevented jackals, hyaenas and other wild animals from unearthing the corpse, and it marked the position of the tomb for the relatives of the deceased, who were expected to come at intervals and bring him fresh provisions.

As far back as the beginning of history the tumulus had developed into a rectangular construction of sun-baked bricks resembling the shape of a house or, in a royal tomb, a palace. The outside walls were ornamented with a continuous series of narrow vertical recesses alternating with projections of the same type. In modern times the Arabic term "mastaba" ("bench") has been applied to tombs of this shape.

In the protodynastic royal tombs at Abydos the bodies lay in a room under the centre of the superstructure, while all around were grouped smaller rooms containing supplies and bodies of male and female servants, who were probably killed at the funeral ceremony to accompany their master into the life beyond. This barbarous custom was early discarded.

Building with stone was introduced at the time of Djoser in the IIIrd Dynasty so that the tomb might be "everlasting". This king had a large stone mastaba constructed on which were piled five other mastabas gradually decreasing in size, so that the whole structure very much resembled a pyramid with steps. With the accession to the throne of the IVth Dynasty a new and definite form was given to the royal tomb, namely that of a true pyramid. Its ground plan was made square, the steps were filled up with stones, the sides became straight and a point was added at the top. It seems that this change from the step-pyramid to a true pyramid was due to the victory of the Heliopolitan solar cult and that the pyramid form was inspired by the *benben*, a high-pointed conical stone worshipped at Heliopolis as the seat of the sun, whose rays when it rose in the morning first caught the point of the *benben*.

All around the pyramid the mastabas of members of the royal family, courtiers and officials were set at a respectful distance, symmetrically arranged in rows, with regular streets running between them from north to south and from east to west. All these mastabas were built of stone, with slightly sloping sides and without any external decoration. The whole town of the dead, surrounded by a wall with the pyramid as its centre, was a replica of the court of a living king.

The entrance to the pyramid lay in its northern side near ground level. From there a passage led to the burial chamber situated either in the rock under the pyramid or in the body of the pyramid itself. In front of the pyramid on the east side lay a funerary temple where the cult of the dead king was celebrated. It consisted of several rooms, some of them accessible to the public, others only to priests. From the temple a covered stone causeway descended to the valley to a massive stone gate on the fringe of the cultivated land.

Access to the burial chamber under the mastaba was through a vertical shaft opening in the flat top of the mastaba. This shaft was filled up with stones and rubble after the burial. For the funerary cult a small brick building was attached to the mastaba on its east side near the south-east corner. It was entered from the north and was divided into two compartments, the more eastern being a store-room with supplies and the more western, which joined the mastaba, a chapel. In the west wall of this chapel, sunk in the face of the mastaba, was a rectangular tablet of stone on which was carved a representation of the deceased sitting at a meal before an offering-table. In the course of time a niche replaced the tablet; eventually this niche was given the form of a "false door" through which, it was believed, the deceased could leave the spirit world of the mastaba and enter the tomb chapel to enjoy the offerings deposited on a stone offering-plate placed in front of the "false door".

In the Vth Dynasty the chapel was transferred from the outside of the mastaba to its interior. Gradually further rooms were added and the false door was placed in the innermost one. In many mastabas, especially the later ones, a special room is found entirely separated by a wall from the other rooms. This room is now known by the Arabic name *serdab* meaning "cellar". The Egyptians called it the "statue house", a term which sufficiently describes its purposes: in it the statue or statues of the deceased were deposited as a seat for his *ka*. The only communication between the *serdab* and the chapel were squints in the intervening wall. They were called "eyes of the *ka*-house" and enabled the dead to see the light of day, to watch the ceremonies performed in the chapel and to enjoy the scent of the burning incense.

The pyramid remained the standard form of a royal tomb until the sixteenth century B.C. But long before that date it had been adopted by commoners, who carved their tombs in the rocks which lie east and west of the Nile. For these tombs the essential elements of an Egyptian house were retained. First a ramp led uphill to an open courtyard, often with a colonnade on the far side; beyond lay a wide covered hall cut in the rock, also with pillars or columns, corresponding to the guest-room of the house. Sometimes a deep, narrow room, called the "long room", intervened between the side room and the small square room at the end, which was the chapel with a statue of the deceased. In this chapel offerings were made to the spirit of the owner; it was a counterpart of the dining-room in his earthly house. A shaft or sloping passage to the underground burial chamber generally led from one of these rooms, less frequently it had its mouth in the courtyard. It was, of course, left to the imagination of the architect or the wealth of the owner to change this plan in points of detail or to add further rooms, but the parts enumerated remained the main elements of a tomb throughout the New Kingdom.

Immediately behind the courtyard, and above the rockhewn rooms, a pyramid was often erected in unbaked bricks. Although it owed its inspiration to the royal pyramids it cannot be compared with them in size, and the angle of its slope is steeper. It is also found above the chapel of those tombs which were not cut in the rock, but were built entirely of brick or stones. The pyramid was painted white to imitate limestone and a limestone point, the pyramidion, was placed on its apex. On the four sides of the pyramidion the deceased was represented in relief adoring the sun-god and the same design was repeated on a stela built into a niche half-way up in the centre of the eastern side of the pyramid.

Tuthmosis I was the first king to abandon the pyramid form for unknown reasons and to initiate a new type of royal tomb which continued to be used from the XVIIIth to XXth Dynasty. In the desert "Valley of Kings" on the west side of Thebes he had his tomb cut in the rock. It consisted of only two relatively small chambers. Subsequent kings considerably enlarged the dimensions of their tombs transforming them into a series of halls and long subterranean passages ending far inside the rock in a pillared chamber in which their stone sarcophagi and their treasures lay.

From the time of Haremhab onwards the royal tombs are cut with their main axis in a straight line. It is not known whether the change in the direction of the axis to the left, first in a curve, later at a right angle, which took place during the XVIIIth Dynasty was for religious or other reasons; in the tombs of Tuthmosis IV and Amenhotep III the axis shows two changes of direction while that of the tomb of Tutankhamun turns abruptly to the right.

The entrances to these tombs were blocked with stones immediately after the burial; in most cases they probably became indistinguishable from the surrounding stones and gravel. In the narrow "Valley of Kings" there was no room for funerary temples; they therefore ceased to be part of the tomb and were erected far away in the Nile Valley on the desert plain extending between the cultivated land and the mountains on the left bank of the Nile.

The kings of the XXIst and subsequent dynasties, who lived at Tanis in the Delta, were buried in crypts under the pavement of a temple in their capital, and so were the kings of the XXVIth Dynasty in Sais, according to Greek authors.

Egyptians spared no effort and expense to ensure a regular performance of the funerary ritual and regular supplies of provisions which they believed necessary for the "eternal" duration of their tombs and for the continuation of life after death. Experience showed that filial gratitude alone could not be relied upon. If some care could reasonably be expected from sons and daughters, perhaps also from grand-children, it was unlikely that the same care would be forthcoming from remoter descendants who had no personal knowledge of their dead ancestor. They would naturally concentrate on their own tombs and funerary cult.

The maintenance of the tomb and of the funerary cult was therefore transferred to persons who were ready to look after the interests of the dead in return for revenues from a funerary foundation. In many cases these persons were sons of the tomb-owner, but in this way the funerary cult was placed on a firm legal basis. The Egyptian reserved a certain part of his fortune for the establishment of a funerary endowment and the revenues of this foundation provided him with his funerary offerings. A part of the revenues, however, went to the "servants of the *ka*" who undertook to maintain the tomb and perform the funerary ritual of offering bread and pouring water before the statue of the deceased. They could bequeath their rights and duties to their descendants.

Under the Old Kingdom owners employed as many funerary priests as they could afford. Since, however, when there were several funerary priests they were apt to quarrel among themselves, the practice of the Middle Kingdom and subsequent periods was to limit the rights and services to one single "servant of the *ka*", well paid, but having in his turn the right to bequeath the office to only one of his children. This practice prevented a progressive division of the revenues of the foundation with the consequent dwindling of the funerary services.

Similar arrangements were made with "lector priests" for reading the liturgy on certain festival days, of which the first and the fifteenth days of the month seem to have been the most important. Sometimes real contracts were made between the owner of the tomb and his funerary priest and the terms were engraved on the walls of the tomb or on a stela. It was even possible for one priest to make agreements of this nature with several tomb owners, so that the office of "servant of the *ka*" became a profession.

The "servant of the *ka*" was in charge of the statue of the deceased, to which he brought offerings consisting of food, chiefly bread and beer, but also meat. This he did on certain days, among which, besides the two mentioned above, New Year's Eve and day, and the eve and day of the *Wag*-festival (on the eighteenth day of the first month of the Egyptian year) were of importance. The offerings were accompanied by the lighting of a candle before the statue so that its owner might see the offerings, and by prayers called "glorifications".

At some time not later than the Middle Kingdom a concession began to be granted by the king, and by him only, to people of some importance and merit, to set up their statues in the courtyards of temples. In this way the person to whom the statue was dedicated participated in the prayers and offerings presented to the god by visitors. Sometimes also contracts were made with the priests of such temples to perform the ritual before the statue on festival days.

The priests appointed for the cult of the kings of the Vth Dynasty in their funerary temples situated on the east side of the pyramids were numerous. They fall into two classes, each under an "instructor" (*sahdj*): "Servants of the god" and *wēeb*-priests (lit. "pure ones"). Besides taking part in the royal cult, the *wēeb*-priests officiated at special sanctuaries of the sun-god Rē, built by most kings of that Dynasty. The term *wēeb*, "pure one" points to a purification or ablution which such priests had to undergo. Since the ritual of purification originated in Heliopolis it is probable that *wēeb*-priests, as a class, had their origin at the Heliopolitan temple of Rē, spreading thence not only into the Rē-cult outside Heliopolis, but also into the funerary cult of the king, who, from the Vth Dynasty onwards, was brought into close relation to Rē as his son.

A noteworthy feature of the Vth Dynasty sun temples is that they are the only Egyptian temples of the Old Kingdom of which an actual example has come down to us and has been excavated. This is the sun temple of Neuserrē at Abusîr. It shows that sun temples were unlike more recent temples of any god in their character and disposition.

From a gateway in the Nile Valley a covered causeway led up to another gate on the desert plateau and to the temple built on an artificial platform. The temple comprised a vast rectangular courtyard, on the west side of which stood a conical base built of huge stones, on which an obelisk of limestone blocks was erected. Opposite the east side of the base lay an altar consisting of five blocks of alabaster. The northern part of the courtyard was occupied by a slaughter-house. Its pavement had a number of parallel runnels through which the blood of the slaughtered animals flowed into ten basins placed along the east side of the slaughter-house. Two corridors led from the upper gate, one to the right to a row of storerooms in the north of the enclosure, the other to the left, first to a vestry at the base of the obelisk and then through the base up on to a platform at the bottom of the obelisk. A wooden boat about 30 m. long resting on a base of bricks to the south of the temple was undoubtedly a material representation of one of the two boats in which the sun was believed to make its daily journey through the sky. Although the area round the temple was carefully examined, no trace of a second boat, which might have been expected, was found.

The whole temple with its courtyard and obelisk faced east towards the rising sun. It was open to the rays of the sun; the point of the obelisk, like the point of the pyramid, was supposed to be the seat of the sun-god.

The reason why the sun-temple differs from the temples of other gods is probably because it imitated in its arrangement the temple of Rē at Heliopolis. There, too, an obelisk called *benben*, erected on a sand-hill, was the central feature of the temple and the seat of the sun-god, who was not represented by a statue as other gods were.

The resemblance of the plan of a normal Egyptian temple of the Middle or New Kingdom to that of an upper-class Egyptian house or royal palace is striking, but not surprising in view of the very human conception of their gods which the Egyptians entertained.

The temple, like the house, stood in the middle of a large rectangular space enclosed by a high wall of sun-dried bricks and entered through a gate guarded by two massive towers, called pylons. Behind the pylons lay, first, a large open courtyard surrounded by colonnades on three sides. An altar was sometimes found in the centre of the courtyard, this altar being an innovation introduced by the solar cult. From the courtyard the visitor entered a hypostyle hall of the same width as the rest of the temple, but not very deep. This "broad hall" was covered by a ceiling supported on columns. Light was admitted through small windows placed high up under the ceiling. The last part of the temple, the sanctuary, was a narrow, deep room, without windows and therefore dark. This was the private apartment of the god accessible only to the king and to the officiating priest or priests. The figure of

H

the god was hidden in a shrine (naos) placed on a boat, both of which were made either of wood or stone. All around the sanctuary were situated other rooms containing the god's treasures and provisions of food, cloth and perfumes. The space between the temple building and the enclosure wall was occupied by the dwellings of the clergy, various workshops, gardens and a sacred lake.

The foundation of a temple was marked by a ceremony called "extending of the measuring-cord", so named after its first and evidently most important part. The protagonist was the king, or in his absence "the chief lector priest and scribe of sacred books", who were supposed to be helped by gods, especially the goddess of learning, Seshat.

The king, followed by his retinue, drove a stake into the ground at each of the four corners of the site of the future temple with a mallet and connected them with a cord, thus marking the area of the temple. Its position had been astronomically fixed on the night before the ceremony by orienting the short axis of the temple from north to south between the constellations of the Great Bear and Orion. Offerings consisting of the heads of a goose and a bull were then brought and placed in a hollow in the ground. The king, kneeling on the ground, sprinkled them with water from two spherical vases. Four bricks for the four corners of the temple were then made by the king himself, who knelt and held the handle of the wooden brick-frame in one hand, while he filled the frame with mud with his other hand.

A preliminary to the laying of the foundations followed, at which the king dug a ditch or channel with a wooden hoe on the four sides of the temple until he reached the level of the subterranean water seeping through from the Nile. He then filled the ditch with sand mixed with sherds, according to the Egyptian practice when building walls; the sand protected the walls against the infiltration of water. Finally, the ceremony was closed by laying the first bricks at the four corners of the temple. At various points foundation deposits consisting of small models of brickmakers' and carpenters' tools and implements were buried under the walls.

This ceremony was undoubtedly very old. It was designed

for buildings made of bricks and wood, and is, therefore, probably anterior in origin to the introduction of building in stone.

When the building was completed another rite took place. The king, carrying a long stick and a mace, "whitewashed" the building with *besen*, probably chalk, a performance which at later periods symbolically represented purification. Then the temple was handed over to the god. This handing over was repeated every year at a ceremony on New Year's Eve when candles were lit and the "house was given to its master". By another rite of consecration a mysterious *life* was imparted to the statues of the temple, to the temple itself as a whole and to its reliefs and religious furnishings. This consisted of the rite of Opening the Mouth performed in every room of the temple. This *life* was renewed every day by the daily temple liturgy. It was further insured by inscribing the formulae of the rite on the walls of the temple. The consecration was followed by a festival meal offered to the craftsmen who had been engaged in building and decorating the temple and to the priests.

The only person who is represented in the temple reliefs and inscriptions as having intercourse with gods is the king, He himself was a god, or the son of a god, and was, therefore, entitled to mediate between the gods, his kin, and the human beings over whom he ruled. But although the king is so represented throughout Egyptian history down to the third century A.D. it is clear that such a state of affairs is a mere fiction and could correspond to reality only in the prehistoric period in a city-state of small extent. There the local chief was naturally also the priest of the city's god. In the two states comprising Upper and Lower Egypt, each including many towns with their various deities, the king, while he remained theoretically chief priest uniting in his person the offices of the former local chiefs, was unable to perform in person his manifold religious functions and had to nominate other persons to do so on his behalf.

The original local divergences with differing local conditions manifested themselves in a great variety of titles borne by the priests of the various gods. A certain number of them survived well into historical times, *e.g.*, "the greatest among the seers (of the god)", title of the chief priest of Rē[1], "the greatest among those who direct crafts", title of the high priest of Ptah, or "the greatest of Five in the House of Thoth", the title of the high priest of Thoth at Hermopolis.

The regular Egyptian word for priests was *hom* "servant". Later we find *hom-neter* "servant of the god". These two together with *wēeb* "pure ones", whose probable origin in the sun-cult has already been mentioned, form the two main categories of the Egyptian priesthood in all historical periods. There is still another class comprising persons called *yot-neter* "father of the god". In the sacerdotal hierarchy they rank between the "servants of the god" and the "pure ones", but neither the reason of their title nor the exact character of their function has so far been satisfactorily explained.

In the Old and Middle Kingdoms the priests were very much like secular officials and were appointed by the king. It was only in the New Kingdom that they formed a definite class in which the sacerdotal office became hereditary. At that time, it seems, the "servants of the god" were professional priests, while the "pure ones" were laymen whose functions were limited to the privilege of carrying the statue of the god in public procession. This is borne out by the fact that the Greeks translated "servant of the god" by *prophētēs*, thus referring to his function of interpreting the god's will; the term "pure one" was translated by the Greek work *hiereus*, but the function of the "pure ones" corresponds at that period to that of *pastophoroi*, "carriers of sacred cells (containing the statue of the god)".

The two subdivisions of professional and lay clergy continued down to Christian times. The former are called in Coptic *hont*, which is a late form of the ancient *hom-neter*; the word designates in Coptic only pagan priests, while *wēeb* "pure" denotes also Christian priests. This difference can perhaps be explained by assuming that the professional class adhered everywhere stubbornly to the old religion, while in the lay element of "pure ones" Christianity took root easily and perhaps even recruited from their ranks most of its own clergy.

In the liturgy the chief officiant was the "servant of the

[1]Another translation suggested for this title is "He who sees the Great One".

god". The spells were recited by the "lector-priest" (*Kher-hebet*, lit. "he who is in charge of the book of festival cere-monies"). *Sem*-priests, found only among clergy of certain gods, seem to be the least important and quite silent: their duty was to carry and present offerings and to raise their arms in a prescribed position.

Accounts and diaries found at Illahun afford us more detailed information as to the organization of the mortuary temple of Senwosret III, which was situated in that locality. The staff permanently in office (*kenbet*) comprised the "chief servant of the god", an "announcer", "master of mysteries", "wardrobe-keeper", "master of the wide hall", "overseer of the chapel of the *ka*", "scribe of the temple", "scribe of the altar" and the "lector-priest"; these functionaries were, therefore, mostly administrative officials. The rest of the priests, the so-called "hour-priests", formed four groups (in Egyptian *sa*, in Greek times called *phylē*, both words meaning "*watch*"), each in turn serving for one month in the temple; when the fourth *phylē* ended its term, the first *phylē* returned, so that the mem-bers of a *phylē* served altogether three months in the year. It was only in the Ptolemaic period that a fifth *phylē* was created. The priest in service was spoken of as "he who is in his month".

The power of the priests of a particular god corresponded to the wealth of his temple. The greatest political power was acquired in the New Kingdom by the clergy of Amun, headed by the "first priest" of Amun, who eventually, under the kings of the XXIst Dynasty, who lived at Tanis in the Delta, suc-ceeded in creating a "state within a state" in Thebes and its neighbourhood. This state was in theory ruled by the god Amun; in practice, however, it was ruled by the high priests themselves, who even wrote their names in cartouches like Egyptian kings and assumed royal titles, though they reckoned the date in terms of the years of the Tanite kings and thus recognized at least a theoretical allegiance to them.

Temple revenues consisted of taxes paid by the inhabitants of the locality in which the temple was situated, and were swelled by gifts of land, cattle and serfs or prisoners of war from the king. In the Middle Kingdom, for instance, every citizen of Siut gave the first-fruit of the harvest to the local temple of

Upuaut. The royal gifts were either the permanent income of the landed property of the temple, or occasional gifts of revenue from certain lands, or a share of booty brought from military expeditions. Through gifts of land in perpetuity the temples became some of the most important landowners of the country: towards the beginning of the XXth Dynasty, the temple of Amun possessed about twenty per cent of all the agricultural land in Egypt, a fact which accounts for the enormous economic and political power of the clergy and high priests of Amun. Other privileges were bestowed on temples by royal decrees: they and their priests were exempted from paying taxes to the treasury, their priests and serfs were relieved of the duty of working on royal lands, and the temple and its property were excluded from the authority of royal officials.

In theory, any revenue or income from the property of the temple, especially the food, drink, clothes and perfumes, belonged to the deity of the temple and went towards his offerings. They were certainly presented to the god, but "after the god was satisfied with them" (as the Egyptian expression puts it) they were divided among the priests and other employees of the temple. It was contrary to the practical sense of the Egyptians to destroy offerings by burning them; holocausts of gazelles, or of geese and goats, however, occurred and the burning of these animals symbolized the destruction of god's enemies. The rite—called "placing a furnace (on fire)"—may be a survival of an early, more general, funeral practice; it is attested as such in the Old Kingdom and goats and geese were in fact the animals slaughtered as offerings, for example, in the very old ceremony of the "Opening of the Mouth".

The hallmark of the priests, namely the purity of the body, was attained by ablutions, chewing natron and depilation, though complete shaving of the head is found only in the New Kingdom and later. Their dress was more conservative than that of other persons and certain food, such as fish, was forbidden to them.

Women seem to have taken no part in the liturgy proper, their role being limited to singing, dancing and performing music in the temple and at the appearances of the god in public during processions. As priests were "servants" of the god, so these women musicians impersonated the god's harim and their leader was regarded as the wife of the god. This wife was in every case supposed to be the goddess Hathor, evidently under the influence of the sun-cult of Heliopolis in which Hathor was the sun-god's wife. At Thebes the chief-priestess of Amun was actually called "God's Wife" and from the XXIIIrd to XXVIth Dynasties five successive wives of the god ruled the sacerdotal state of Thebes.

From what has been said so far about the liturgy it will be clear that the temple ritual was performed by a few priests in the innermost sanctuary of the temple, to which the general public had no access. The latter were admitted only as far as the open court where they could "pour water" as a libation to the god and pronounce a prayer. The only opportunity which the masses were allowed of coming into the vicinity of a god was during the festivals called "coming forth", when the statue of the god, carried in procession, left its own sanctuary to pay a visit to another god in the same town or in another locality. These processions originated in the belief that the god, like a human being, was entitled to pleasures and enjoyed a trip or a visit; later they were presented as repetitions of an event in the mythological history of the god. Some festivals were purely local, others, however, had a wide reputation and attracted crowds from near and far. Herodotus' account of the festival of the goddess—Bastet at Bubastis should be read as a vivid description of a solemn event of this kind.

The festival of a god was either attached to a season or to a date in the civil year which generally bore no relation to the seasons, according to the nature of the god in question. Several "comings forth of Min", the god of fertility, were celebrated throughout the country in his temples, the most important festival taking place at the beginning of the harvest. The statue of Min was carried on poles by priests, all of whom were wrapped in a large canopy adorned with the king's names so that only the heads and feet of the priests projected from above and below the canopy. A smaller group of priests followed carrying bundles of lettuces, the plant sacred to Min. A white bull was also led in the procession and images of kings and the ensigns of gods were carried on staffs. When the god was installed upon his throne, called the "stairway", under a baldachin, offerings were brought, an ear of grain was cut for the god and four birds released to the four cardinal points of the compass with written proclamations of the festival.

Two festivals of Amun had their origin at Thebes and always remained purely local, though owing to their great popularity the months in which they were celebrated were later named after them, thus spreading the names of the two feasts all over the country.

The "festival of Opet" began on the nineteenth day of the second month of the year and lasted for twenty-seven days at the time of Ramesses III. It seems to have been purely an excursion of Amun, Mut and Khons from their temples at Karnak to Luxor (Egn. Opet) and back. All three deities travelled in their ceremonial barques on the Nile, Amun's barque being towed by that of the king and this in turn by smaller barques rowed by high officials. During the whole journey incense was burnt before the statues of the deities and fans held above them. They were accompanied, both on the river and on land, by a huge crowd consisting of the inhabitants of Thebes, the army, priests and male and female singers. When the procession entered the temple of Luxor various offerings were brought, especially oxen fattened for the occasion, and the smaller barques in which the deities had been carried on land were placed in special chapels. After remaining there for some time they were taken back to Karnak to their respective temples, making the journey in exactly the same way as they had made the journey to Luxor.

At the "Feast of the Valley" in the tenth month of the year, Amun—alone this time—crossed the Nile in his barque and visited the funerary temples of the kings on the west bank to "pour water for the kings of Upper and Lower Egypt". The ultimate goal of his journey was the "Valley", that is the valley of Der el-Bahari where the mortuary temple of Queen Hatshepsut was situated, which was also a temple of Hathor.

During the processions of certain gods scenes were sometimes performed from the mythological history of the god after the manner of the Greek mysteries, though access to them may not have been limited to a narrow circle of privileged and initiated persons. The mysteries of Osiris at Abydos were renowned but very few details are known apart from the mere fact of their existence. These details are chiefly derived from an inscription on the grave stela of the chief treasurer, Ikhernofret, who was sent to Abydos by Senwosret III to reorganize the cult of Osiris and to restore the image of the god and other furnishings of his temple. During his stay at Abydos he attended the religious plays there. They began with the appearance of the statue of Upuaut, which preceded that of Osiris in order to make the way safe; Osiris followed in his barge called *neshemet*, smiting his enemies. In this part of the ceremony the spectators fought with another party representing the enemies of the god. Then in a "great coming forth" Osiris went to be killed by Sētekh; the actual death, if acted at all, probably took place in secret. Several days of general mourning followed. The figure of Osiris was decked with funeral ornaments and a wreath and then carried in another barque for burial in a district called *Peker*, about 2 kilometres south-east of the temple of Osiris, where the actual tomb of Osiris was believed to lie. A crowd accompanied the god; litanies and praise were sung: offerings were brought, and they and the wreaths removed from the image of the god were divided among the participants. Nedit, the place where, according to the myth, Osiris had been killed, was somewhere in the vicinity of Abydos and there a second encounter was enacted in which Sētekh and his followers were overcome and thus the murder of Osiris was avenged. The *neshemet* barque with Osiris risen and triumphant was finally conducted back to the temple amid the general rejoicings of the assembled multitude.

Some of the gods were actually hidden even during the processions in public. Thus, while the statue of Min was uncovered and visible to everybody in the god's "coming forth" described above, the statues of Amun, Mut and Khons were concealed in small wooden shrines (Greek *naos*) mounted on the barques. The door—to judge from the numerous scenes of processions represented in relief and in paintings that have come down to us—seems to have been covered by a curtain. Despite this invisibility, contact with the god was felt to be so close that gods were petitioned during their appearance, like the king or high officials. People were allowed to stand up before the barque of the deity when it halted and to address questions to him which he answered in an oracular fashion.

Certain dates were reserved for festivals in honour of the dead, when offerings were brought, lights kindled and "glorifications" recited before the statues of deceased persons, which were either erected as a privilege in temples to participate in offerings and prayers presented to the gods, or placed in the chapels of the tombs in charge of the mortuary priests. Most of these funerary festivals took place towards the end and at the beginning of the year, especially on the first intercalary day (i.e., the 361st day of the year), New Year's Eve, New Year's Day and the Wag Festival.

It is impossible to conclude an account of Egyptian festivals without paying some attention to a festival which has remained until recently entirely obscure and concerning which some rather fantastic and far-fetched explanations have been suggested. This is the "Sed-festival", one of the oldest feasts, the origin of which goes back to the very beginning of Egyptian history. It was celebrated by some kings after they had reigned for thirty years and subsequently repeated every three years. Other kings, however, celebrated it although it is certain that they never reigned so long; perhaps they counted their years from the time when they became crown-princes. The real character of the festival was a periodical re-enactment of the union of Egypt by the conquest of Lower Egypt, first accomplished by Menes and thenceforward represented symbolically by every king at the moment of ascending the throne.

The Sed-festival was celebrated at Memphis; in the Ramesside period it was placed under the auspices of Ptah, though gods and goddesses with their priests were summoned from all parts of the country to tender their congratulations to the king on his jubilee. The statues or emblems of the divine guests were housed in two rows of shrines or chapels on opposite sides of a large court. Another festival court built especially for the occasion had as its most prominent feature two large thrones for the king under a canopy standing on a high platform reached by two flights of steps. A further building, a temporary palace, contained robing rooms where the king dressed and changed for various stages of the festival.

The festival seems to have begun on the first day of the fourth month of the year, but its duration is unknown. The protagonist was the king, the queen took no part in the ceremony. At the beginning, the king accompanied by officials paid a visit on foot to the local gods and presented them with offerings. In a second ceremony he walked to the double throne preceded by the ensign of the god Upuaut of Siut, who played an important part in the festival and whose nome had been an important ally of the King of Hierakonpolis in the fight for the first union of Egypt. The king sat down alternately on each of the two thrones and his first coronation as King of Upper and Lower Egypt was re-enacted. He was wrapped in a half-length cloak and held a sceptre, the symbol of his royal power. Sitting on the throne he received the allegiance of his subjects and the blessings of the gods through the persons of their priests, the gods receiving offering in return.

Next followed an offering dance which seems to have been the climax of the festival. The king took off the cloak and, dressed only in a short kilt with an animal's tail hanging behind, the crown of Upper Egypt on his head and a short sceptre and a whisk in his hands, he ran four ritual courses offering to Upuaut his royal insignia.

In the final stage a palanquin was brought before the throne and the king, wrapped in a cloak of a very fine fabric, mounted and was carried away in a great procession to visit the chapels of the gods Horus and Sētekh. These handed over to him four arrows of victory which the king directed towards the four cardinal points of the compass to smite his enemies.

CHAPTER V

EGYPTIAN AND FOREIGN GODS.
DECLINE OF EGYPTIAN RELIGION

TOLERANCE is a feature common to all polytheistic religions, and the Egyptians extended the same hospitality to foreign gods as they did to any other foreigners who desired to settle in their country. It is, however, remarkable that during the Old and Middle Kingdoms only one foreign god is found taking advantage of this hospitality. The reason for this was undoubtedly that the religions of Nubia, Libya, the Sinai peninsula and southern Palestine, which bordered on Egypt, could offer no deities impressive and powerful enough to establish themselves in Egypt side by side with the native gods and to be accepted as equals in their company and in the religious feeling of the Egyptians.

The one exception is the Nubian god Dedun, who is mentioned several times as an incense bringer, and is called "the Upper Egyptian youth who has come from To-Seti (Nubia)" in the Pyramid inscriptions of the kings of the VIth Dynasty. In the earlier version of the Vth Dynasty his name does not yet occur, and we may conclude that he was a newcomer to the Egyptian pantheon at the beginning of the VIth Dynasty, as a result of the important position which Nubia held in the flourishing trade of the time as the transmitter of merchandise from countries lying farther to the south. In later times Dedun appeared as a subordinate divinity on monuments at various places in Egypt, but not north of Thebes.

The Libyan origin of the god Ash is doubtful, though he is attested in the IInd Dynasty, and on one later occasion he is called "Lord of Tjehenu (Libya)". He may be a local god of some frontier district of Egypt claiming rule over the adjacent foreign land, as the goddess Neith of Sais did over Libya and the god Sopd of Saft el-Henna in the eastern Delta over the eastern countries.

When the Egyptians became acquainted with some foreign

deity on their travels, they seem usually to have been reminded of an Egyptian god or goddess of similar character with whom they then identified the foreign one. The sky goddess, Hathor, was singularly well suited to stand for most female deities abroad, especially in Asia. There, in the Syrian port of Byblos, Egyptian traders at a very early date met a great Syrian goddess whom they called "Hathor, Lady of Byblos". She was the patroness of sailors, while at another place on the Sinai peninsula the great goddess had become "Hathor, Lady of the Turquoise" after the chief product which the Egyptians sought in the Sinai mountains. Hathor, Lady of Byblos became popular in Egypt also.

Similarly, in the warlike male gods of Palestine and Syria they saw their own god Sētekh, the mythological adversary of Horus, who was himself incarnate in the Egyptian king. And while according to the ancient myth the fight between Horus and Sētekh was stopped by assigning Lower and Upper Egypt to them respectively, there was another version according to which the whole of the "Black Land" (Egypt) had been given to Horus, while the "Red Lands", that is, foreign countries, had been given to Sētekh.

There is no sign that the cult of any specifically Egyptian god was introduced in a temple built for him outside Egypt before the end of the Middle Kingdom, except in Nubia, which was conquered by the first kings of the XIIth Dynasty. Side by side with the construction of fortresses and Egyptian settlements and the establishment of Egyptian administration there, the god of the Cataract region, Khnum, was introduced in the newly built temples, though the native god Dedun continued to play a minor part in them in Khnum's company.

But while hardly any foreign god can be traced in Egypt during the Old and Middle Kingdom, this state of affairs changed greatly in the New Kingdom. The Pharaohs of the XVIIIth Dynasty established a permanent empire in Asia, the frontiers of which at one time reached the banks of the Euphrates. The Egyptians found everywhere Semitic city states which had been under strong Babylonian influence and enjoyed a high degree of civilization, and they made the acquaintance of a great multitude of town gods and goddesses called Baʻal (Semitic "Lord") and Baʻalat ("Mistress"). From the conquered territories large numbers of prisoners were brought to Egypt and settled there as slaves on the temple and crown estates. These were followed by voluntary immigrants, craftsmen, traders and soldiers, who often reached high and influential positions at court, in the administration or in the army. They all brought to Egypt the worship of their native gods to whom they built sanctuaries in the country of their adoption. It became the fashion among the Egyptians themselves to imitate Asiatic customs, Semitic words penetrated by the score into the language, and with them spread the cult of the foreign gods of the newcomers, various Baʻals and Baʻalats, under their specific names of Mikal and Reshep (or better Ershōp), and the worship of the goddesses Astarte, Anat, Kadesh, Kesret and others.

The Pharaohs themselves took the lead in this. In Egypt the king was presented in every temple and sanctuary as the son of the local god or goddess; and the Egyptian administration and garrisons naturally applied this same conception in various sanctuaries in the Asiatic provinces where they were stationed. Thus Amenhotep II is "beloved of Ershōp" who "rejoiced" over him while he was still a crown prince, and so did the goddess Astarte, impersonating the generating power. Ramesses II is said to be the "suckling" of the warlike goddess Anat, while Anat and Astarte were "shields" to Ramesses III and protected the chariot of the king. It is, therefore, a great compliment for Tuthmosis IV to be called "strong horseman like Astarte". A group of statues show Ramesses II sitting on the right side of Anat, who is represented with her hand on the king's shoulder saying, "I am thy mother".

Since these divinities stood in such close relationship to Pharaoh we are not surprised to find the Egyptian officials and soldiers in the cities of Palestine and Syria approaching them with the same confidence as they displayed towards their own home gods. The builder Amenemōpe, under Tuthmosis III, erected a stela in the temple at Bethshan in Palestine to Mikal "Lord of Bethshan", "the great god"; in the time of Amenhotep III an Egyptian lady dedicated a stela to Astarte in the same sanctuary, and another Egyptian, under Ramesses II, set up a stela to Anat. At Ras-Shamra in Syria a stela was dedicated by Memi to Baʿal-zephon ("Baʿal of the North").

The centre of the worship of the Asiatic gods in Egypt was Memphis, where personal names composed with the names of these gods are found in the New Kingdom. Under the XVIIIth Dynasty a quarter of the town was called the "district of Hittites", and this is presumably identical with the "Camp of the Tyrians" mentioned later by Herodotus as the seat of the "foreign Aphrodite", that is, the un-Egyptian Astarte. An Egyptian papyrus enumerating Memphite deities of Egyptian origin also contains side by side with them the names of "Baʿalat, Kadesh, Anyt and Baʿal-zephon", all probably housed in that district not far from the temple of Ptah. Owing to this proximity Astarte became the "daughter of Ptah" in one Egyptian tale, while in another she and Anat were "daughters of Rē", and Ershōp received the epithet "he who listens to prayers", which is usually applied to Ptah. Furthermore, Ershōp is "great god", and Anat, Kadesh and Astarte all bear the title "Mistress of the sky, lady of the gods" like Egyptian divinities, though in representations they keep their foreign appearance: Ershōp, with a high conical cap on his head ending in a long tassel, holds a shield and a spear in his left hand and a mace in his right; Astarte, bearing a shield and a mace, rides on horseback, an entirely un-Egyptian habit; Kadesh stands naked on a lion and holds flowers in one hand and a snake in the other. Priests ("prophets") of these divinities are attested in Memphis, though the earliest known, a prophet of Baʿal and Astarte at the time of Amenhotep IV, is still a foreigner from the Syrian town of Zirbashan.

Ramesses II must have been a zealous worshipper of Anat, for not only did he call his mares after Anat, and his favourite daughter Bint-Anat (Semitic "Daughter of Anat"), but he introduced the worship of Anat in his new Delta residence at Per-Ramesse, later called Tanis, where a temple was even erected to the goddess by the king. At Tanis, Ramesses is also called "beloved of Hauron", a Semitic god about whom very little is known in his original home in Asia. At Tanis he is represented as a falcon, that is Horus, and in Memphis he was connected with the Great Sphinx.

The worship of Semitic deities was not, however, limited to Memphis and its foreign quarter or to the Ramesside residence in the Delta. Ershōp is also found far away in the south in a rock graffito near Toshkah in Nubia, and Ershōp, Anat and Kadesh were quite popular among the working class in the Theban necropolis. Astarte was called Istar in Assyria and Istar of Nineveh was famed for her healing power. She too became known in Egypt and we learn from a cuneiform tablet when and under what circumstances this happened. The tablet is a letter written by Tushratta, King of Mitanni, in which he informs his son-in-law, Amenhotep III, that he is sending to him Istar of Nineveh, by which a statue of the goddess is certainly meant. The letter is dated in Amenhotep III's thirty-sixth year, and the purpose of the goddess's journey is evidently to bring about the Egyptian king's recovery from a grave illness. It seems that the image of the goddess remained in Egypt, for a stela now at Copenhagen, possibly of somewhat later date, was dedicated to a goddess Istar by an Egyptian, Rome by name, who is also represented on the stela. From this representation we can safely guess the reason for the dedication: the man, still young, has a club-foot and hopes to be healed by Istar.

But while the Egyptians so readily accepted Semitic divinities into their midst, there is no sign that their subjects in Palestine and Syria showed the same attitude towards Egyptian gods. Temples to Egyptian gods, such as that of Ramesses III to Amun, were built and objects bearing witness to the worship of Egyptian deities have, of course, been found in sanctuaries of native gods in Palestine and Syria, but these have all been dedicated by Egyptians stationed there as officials or soldiers. It is impossible to adduce a single example of native origin of the cult of an Egyptian deity. Still, they must have been held in some respect there, for even at the end of the XXth Dynasty, at a time when Egyptian influence in Asia had almost completely faded away, the king of Byblos admitted the power of Amun when speaking to Wenamun, an envoy of the high-priest of Amun of Thebes, who had come to Byblos to seek timber for Amun's sacred barque. The king, though denying that he was a servant of the high-priest, declared that "Amun has equipped all lands; he has equipped them, and the land of Egypt he equipped first; for cunning work (*i.e.*, arts and crafts) came forth from it to reach my abode, and teaching (*i.e.*, learning) came forth from it to reach my abode".

In Egypt the widespread popularity of Semitic gods did not succeed in influencing the development of Egyptian religious thought at all, and when once the empire in Asia was lost even their popularity dwindled away very fast. Though the centre of their cult, the foreign quarter at Memphis, persisted down to Ptolemaic times, in which it appears under the name of Astartieion, their names faded from the minds of the Egyptian people and disappeared from Egyptian monuments except for an occasional offering scene before Anat or Astarte, and these may have been thoughtless copies of earlier models.

As to the countries lying west of Egypt, the cult of Sētekh, whom, as we have seen, the Egyptians regarded as the god of foreign lands, penetrated into the oases of the Libyan desert at an early stage and in the oasis of Dakhle his oracle was still flourishing under the XXIInd Dynasty. The largest and most distant of them, however, the oasis of Siwa, had a cult of Amun and was therefore known as the Oasis of Jupiter Ammon in the classical world. Amun also supplanted the cult of Sētekh in the oasis of el-Khargeh.

The temples of Amun both at el-Khargeh and Siwa date from the Persian period, but Amun's cult must have penetrated there several centuries earlier, before the general decline of his worship in Egypt proper. The reputation of the oracle of Jupiter Ammon spread throughout the eastern Mediterranean. Alexander the Great visited the temple in 332 B.C., after his conquest of Egypt. He was greeted by the priests as the son of the god in accordance with Egyptian tradition; this episode proved to be the beginning of the profound change in Alexander's conception of royalty and his own destiny. His conquest of the world was later attributed to a promise by the oracle of Jupiter Ammon.

It was, however, in Nubia and the Sudan, the countries south of Egypt, that the Egyptian religion had the most thorough and lasting influence. The Egyptian conquest under the first kings of the XIIth Dynasty, who pushed their frontier up the Nile as far as the Second Cataract, found Nubia inhabited by

I

nomadic and cattle-breeding tribes with a civilization hardly superior to that of prehistoric Egypt. About the religion of this native population nothing is known beyond the existence of the god Dedun, whom we have already mentioned, and what can be guessed at from the graves and their equipment. In the temples which the conquerors built in the newly founded towns and fortresses Dedun continued to be worshipped, but the Egyptians also introduced their own gods, especially the triad of Elephantine, the god Khnum and the two goddesses Satet and Anuket.

In the Second Intermediate Period Nubia was lost but was quickly reconquered at the beginning of the XVIIIth Dynasty and new territories added to the south as far as the present province of Dongola. The favourite god at this time was in most places Horus, the kingly god, of whom the King of Egypt was the earthly incarnation. There were thus various *"Horuses"* in various Nubian towns, such as *"Horus of Buhen"* (near Wadi Halfa), *"Horus of Miam"* (Aniba), *"Horus of Baki"* (Kuban), *"Horus of Meha"* (Abusimbel). Besides the worship of the royal god Horus, the cults of individual kings were carried on to a much greater degree than in Egypt itself: Senwosret III of the XIIth Dynasty, to whom the first conquest was ascribed, was worshipped in the temples of the fortresses of Semneh and Kumneh; Tuthmosis III, Amenhotep III and his Queen Tiye, Tutankhamun and Ramesses II were also worshipped in various places. But all these royal cults were only subsidiary to the great Egyptian gods Amun of Thebes, Re-Harakhte of Heliopolis and Ptah of Memphis, especially the first.

Tuthmosis III built a temple to "Amun, lord of the thrones of the Two Lands", that is to Amun of Karnak, far to the south at Napata, the present Gebel Barkal, at the foot of a high, flat-topped mountain ("the pure mountain" of the Egyptians) rising steeply from the plain not far from the Nile. The priests of Thebes claimed for their god supremacy over the whole of Nubia, as the Theban priests claimed it for Amun of Karnak over Egypt and her Asiatic dependencies. The colonization of the country was finished and Nubia was outwardly Egyptianized though it is difficult to say how far the Egyptianization affected the nomads.

When Nubia was lost to Egypt is not known, very probably during the time of the sacerdotal state of Amon-Rē at Thebes under the XXIst Dynasty. This god's state in Egypt succumbed to and was replaced by a military state organized from the Lower Egyptian town of Bubastis by kings who were descendants of a mercenary chief of Libyan origin. But Napata became the capital of an independent kingdom of Ethiopia, and while the power of Amun in Egypt rapidly declined, the priest of Amun of Napata maintained in Ethiopia a theocracy in which Amun's oracle at Napata elected kings to the throne and decided their political actions. In about 730 B.C. the will of Amun sent the King Piankhy on an expedition against Egypt, which was split into a number of independent kingdoms at that time. Piankhy conquered the country, sparing the temples throughout Egypt very carefully; he attended in person the festivals of various gods, brought offerings to them and observed their ritual and ceremonies. He considered himself to be a true and orthodox Egyptian and treated the Egyptian dynasts scornfully as impure. In so doing he reflected the attitude of the Ethiopians, who considered themselves the true and unspoiled heirs of the old Egyptian religion and civilization in general, and succeeded in impressing this idea upon the ancient world to such an extent that to the Greeks the Ethiopians were the wisest and the most pious men and Ethiopia the cradle of Egyptian civilization, which was just the reverse of the truth.

Piankhy's conquest was only temporary but his successor, Shabaka, occupied Egypt again and founded the XXVth or Ethiopian Dynasty there. The Ethiopian kings were buried with their queens in pyramids in the royal cemetery near their capital at Napata and their tombs are purely Egyptian in character. Their pyramids, it is true, look strange with their very steep sides, but their burial chambers contained mummies and equipment with which we are familiar in Egypt, such as sarcophagi, ushebtis, canopic jars and scarabs, and their walls were covered with Egyptian funerary representations and inscriptions in hieroglyphic writing. Osiris, Isis and Anubis occur on these monuments beside Amon-Rē'. In short, the religion of the Ethiopians, the official one at least, was Egyptian;

whether all their subjects shared the religious beliefs of their royal masters it is, however, impossible to tell.

When Egypt became independent again under Psammetichus I in 663 B.C., Ethiopia's relations with her were irrevocably severed. The capital of Ethiopia was transferred in the third century B.C. to Meroë, north of Khartûm, and the culture and religion of the country began to degenerate slowly into barbarism.

To return to Egypt, the establishment of the sacerdotal state at Thebes ruled by Amun through his high-priest was the culminating point in the history of Egyptian religion. It had yet another 1,500 years or so to run, but these were to be years of slow but steady decline. The Egyptian religion had lost its vitality and inner power of development; the decline of religion proceeded along parallel lines with the decline in other spheres of national life, political and cultural. The XXIInd Dynasty of Bubastis was a dynasty of Libyan mercenary chiefs who transformed Egypt into a military state. Though all its kings added to their name the old Ramesside epithet "beloved of Amun", they favoured the cult of the goddess Bastet of Bubastis and other gods of the Delta, whose temples lay nearer to their capital. They secured influence in Thebes by appointing their sons as high-priests of Amun there, although the real rulership of the Theban sacerdotal state no longer lay with the high-priests, but with the "god's wife of Amun", Amun's consort on earth. This priestly institution had been created in the XVIIIth Dynasty and was most often filled by a princess. With time it became almost as important as the kingship and high-priesthood of Amun; in the XXIInd Dynasty it overshadowed the latter.

When the kings of Ethiopia conquered Egypt and founded the XXVth Dynasty it seemed at first as if the old days of the glory of Amun were returning. The Ethiopians were themselves fervent worshippers of Amun of Napata in their homeland, and the might of Amun of Napata now strengthened the position of Amun of Thebes. But in 663 B.C., during the wars between Tanutamun, King of Ethiopia, and Assurbanipal, King of Assyria, the Assyrians took Thebes and laid waste the town and its temples. Tanutamun retreated to Ethiopia a few years later never to return to Egypt, and with the departure of the Ethiopians Amun definitely descended to the rank of a local god. He did not even rise again when, soon afterwards, Egypt became independent under the native king, Psammetichus I, and his XXVI Dynasty.

The new Dynasty originated in Sais in the Delta, where its kings lived. Thebes remained a provincial town and the goddess Neith of Sais became the state deity. The high-priest of Amun was by then an insignificant person and such influence as still remained with the "god's wife of Amun" passed into the hands of the new Saite Dynasty in 655 B.C. when the "god's wife" Shepenwepet, daughter of the Ethiopian King Piankhy, was compelled by Psammetichus I to adopt his daughter Nitokre as her daughter and successor.

The Egyptians saw only one remedy for the political decay manifested in the frequent division of the country into small units and in its spiritual decline, and that was a return to the institutions and spiritual life of the past. This process was initiated by the Ethiopian kings who, regarding themselves as the heirs of Egypt, attempted to give her a political unity. In spiritual life, especially in religion and art, they chose as their ideal the Egypt of the glorious days of the Old Kingdom; they probably did not think the New Kingdom a worthy model, since during that period the country was wide open to influences from Asia. Old beliefs and old forms of cult were sought for and it was this archaizing tendency which gave the Egyptian religion and, in fact, the whole of Egyptian life that ancient character which later impressed the Greeks and aroused their admiration.

Under the rule of the indigenous XXVIth Dynasty the archaizing tendencies were marked by complete success. Outwardly, Egypt did indeed resemble the Egypt of the Pyramid builders, and so far this period of its history is entitled to the name of "renaissance" by which it is usually known. But militarily and economically the country was weak and in these spheres Psammetichus I and his successor had to rely on the Greeks; Greek mercenaries garrisoned its frontier fortresses and Greek traders were given a commercial reservation at Naucratis in the Delta. The Greek mercenaries could not save

Egypt from conquest by the Persians in 525 B.C., and the Greek merchants may even have welcomed it, because within the framework of the Persian empire new ways were opened to their trade, and in Egypt itself their settlement was no longer limited to Naucratis. Apart from stationing their own garrisons in Egypt and levying a substantial tax, the Persians changed nothing in the institutions of the country. As regards religion they were tolerant; the temple of Amun in the oasis of el-Khargeh was built under Darius I and inscribed with the name of this king, which would have been impossible without his permission.

Little is known about the attitude of the earlier Greek settlers to the Egyptian religion. Herodotus says that Amasis assigned places for building altars and sanctuaries to the Greeks who were not settled in Egypt, but who merely sailed across on business, and this information must certainly be interpreted in the sense that the Greeks were given the opportunity to worship their own gods. In Naucratis itself excavations have revealed the remains of early temples of Apollo, Hera, Aphrodite, Dioskuroi and a vast temenos of Hellenion founded jointly by a number of Greek communities of Asia Minor, and to these can be added a temple of Zeus the existence of which we know from literary sources. No trace of a sanctuary of any Egyptian deity was found nor any proof that the Greeks of Naucratis adopted any of the Egyptian gods, though the worship of Isis is mentioned there in an inscription probably of the fifth century B.C. But while the attitude of the Greek merchants to the Egyptian religion seems to have been somewhat indifferent, the Egyptian religion, as indeed the country and its civilization as a whole, roused considerable interest and admiration in the Greek intellectuals coming from Greece on visits.

The second book of Herodotus is probably a characteristic example of this interest. He describes various Egyptian cults repeatedly and in great detail and relates their myths and so becomes our chief source for the religion of the Saite and Persian periods. He is not surprised by the worship of animals, and states with approval that in the worship of the gods the Egyptians excelled all other men. Following the example of his countrymen he sees analogies between various Greek and Egyptian deities, analogies which are sometimes based on quite inessential details: to him Osiris is Dionysus, Horus Apollo, Bastet Artemis, Isis Demeter, Amun (or Ammon, as he spells the name) is Zeus. Of other Egyptian gods and goddesses he knew only the equivalent Greek names, such as Ares, Aphrodite, Athene, Hephaestus, Hermes, Heracles, Selene, Typhon, and he believed that these names were of Egyptian origin and had been taken over by the Greeks.

Less fortunate than the Greeks, who could worship their gods unhampered and build sanctuaries to them in the Greek settlements in the Delta, were the Jews. Since the time of the XXVIth Dynasty they had formed a considerable part of the garrison at Elephantine as mercenaries in the fortress defending Egypt from attack in the south. There they were allowed to build a temple to Yahve and his two female companions, Ashima and Anat, whose worship was not forbidden among Jews before the introduction of the unified religious law on the occasion of the rebuilding of Yahve's temple at Jerusalem in 515 B.C. The Jews of Elephantine also continued to enjoy the privilege of possessing a sanctuary of their own during the Persian rule throughout the fifth century; but clashes now and then took place between them and the native Egyptian population, probably as a result of the increase of Egyptian nationalism under foreign domination.

In 410 B.C. the priests of Khnum, having secured the consent of the Persian commander, raised soldiers of Egyptian descent who penetrated into Yahve's temple, pillaged its precious sacred vessels and demolished and burnt the temple. When the Jews complained to the Persian satrap at Memphis, the commander who had agreed to this misdeed was punished by death, but it was only in 407 B.C., after continuous requests and bribery, that the Jews secured from the Persian authorities permission to rebuild the temple. Whether they were ever able to make use of this permission is not known; for shortly afterwards, in 405 B.C., Egypt revolted against the Persians and regained its independence for several decades, and it is likely that the permission to rebuild was revoked at the instance of the Egyptians of Elephantine.

The attitude of the Greeks to the Egyptian religion underwent a fundamental change through the conquest of Egypt by

Alexander in 332 B.C., which changed the status of the Greeks from that of mere settlers to that of the ruling class. Alexander's army was followed by a steadily increasing influx of Greeks from all parts of the Greek world seeking their fortune in the country thus newly opened up. They were no longer limited to a few small settlements, but spread all over the country. Alexandria, which had been recently founded, was entirely Greek in its architecture and population and continued to remain so, developing into the centre of Greek spiritual life of that time; but elsewhere the Greeks faced an overwhelming majority of native population. The conflict between the age-old Egyptian culture and the relatively fresh one of the Greeks began.

In the cemetery of Hermopolis (situated near the present Tuna el-Gebel in Upper Egypt) a great intermingling of Egyptian and Greek art as well as a religious syncretism are shown over practically the whole of the period from the third century B.C. to the third century A.D. The stone temple-tomb of the priest of Thoth, Petosiris, betrays Greek influence in its reliefs very soon after Alexander's conquest; in the two-storeyed funerary houses of sun-baked bricks of Roman date the white-washed walls are covered with scenes from the Greek legends of Agamemnon and Oedipus in one case, and with Horus and Thoth pouring purifying water over a woman dressed in Greek fashion in another.

The Greek colony which settled at Memphis found there the flourishing funerary cult of the Osirified sacred bull Apis, worshipped under the name of Usar-Hape, and they adopted him as Osorapis. The worship of other deities of the Osirian circle, especially Isis and Anubis, was added to that of Osorapis. It was Osorapis of Memphis whom Ptolemy I chose to be the god common to both elements in the country, Egyptian and Greek, which he was anxious to see merged into one nation. The Greek Timotheus and the Egyptian Manehto (Manethos in the Greek form of the name) were consulted as theological representatives and experts of the two nationalities. After their consent had been obtained a statue of the old-new god, to whom the name of Sarapis was given, was imported into Alexandria from Sinope on the northern shore of Asia Minor, and the will of the king enforced the worship of this deity who was

Egyptian by name and origin and Greek in the appearance of his statue. A temple in Greek style, the Serapeum, was built for him at Alexandria by the architect Parmeniscus, which was replaced later under Ptolemy III by another larger and more magnificent. The liturgical language of the new god was Greek.

Sarapis, whom the Egyptians continued to call Usar-Hape, became immensely popular among both Egyptians and Greeks. His appearance was that of the Greek Pluto, the god of the underworld. Seated on a throne, with luxuriant curly hair and a long beard and dressed in a long cloak, he was represented leaning on a long staff which he held in his left hand, while his right hand rested on the triple-headed Cerberus lying at his feet. From Alexandria Sarapis came back to Memphis, where the old cemetery of the sacred bulls was now also called the Serapeum. Gradually his worship spread over the whole land and became the official cult of the empire of the Ptolemies.

The easy victory of Sarapis, a deity who was essentially funerary, becomes more comprehensible when we take into account what was probably the most profound change which had been going on since the New Kingdom in the world of the gods, that is the slow but continuous penetration of Osiris into the realm of the living. He was now no longer concerned only with the dead over whom he had ruled since the time of the Old Kingdom, but assumed the rulership of this world also. In earlier periods it would have been unthinkable, indeed it would probably have been considered an ill omen, to bear a name composed with the name of Osiris, but now names like Petosiris ("He whom Osiris has given") were great favourites. The Apis bull, who in the New Kingdom had been called "repetition of Ptah", became after death so closely associated with Osiris that he eventually merged with him into one deity, Usar-hape. The connection of the Apis with the dead can be observed as early as the Saite period when a representation of an Apis bull running and transporting the dead to the tomb on its back is found at the foot-end of coffins.

With the expansion of Osiris, the cult of the sun-god Rē vanished, and his personality became more and more absorbed by Osiris. As early as the XXth Dynasty the second part of the name of Osiris (-ire) was written by means of the hieroglyph of

the sun-disk instead of the usual image of the eye; this shows
that the idea of the sun-god began to be evoked by the name of
Osiris. In the Ptolemaic period Rē hardly occurs, his role having
been taken over by Osiris. Thus the event foreshadowed by a
text of the XVIIIth Dynasty actually took place; for the text
called Osiris the "ruler who occupied the seat of Rē", that is
became the successor of the sun-god. Isis, too, advanced to the
position of the highest goddess together with Osiris, and in
their son *"Horus, the child"* (*Har-pe-khrad*, in Greek Harpokrates) almost nothing was left of the old solar character, though
his cult was very popular.

The first trace of Egyptian gods in the Greek world is found
towards the end of the fourth century in the cult of Isis and
Ammon in the Piraeus among the Egyptian traders who used
to come and stay there on business. Other mentions of the
worship of Egyptian deities met with on the Greek islands and
in Greek towns in Asia Minor at about the time of the first
Ptolemy have also probably to be ascribed to the Egyptians.
Ptolemy II, who had already secured possession of the Ægean
islands and was conquering the Greek towns on the coast of
Asia Minor, made an attempt to influence their administration.
The officials sent from Egypt for this purpose helped to spread
Egyptian cults there; the cult of Sarapis in Delos is of a somewhat earlier date, but temples were now built to him at Miletus
and Halicarnassus.

From the islands the cult of Egyptian gods easily crossed
to Greece proper; Isis was already established at Athens and
Euboea and was now joined by Sarapis, whose worship was
practised by private societies. On the islands and in Asia, however, the cults of Sarapis and Isis were of a public character;
this was fostered by the Ptolemies, who associated their own
worship as Egyptian rulers with that of Egyptian gods. These
cults were also brought by retiring Greek and Macedonian
officials to their native cities, as we know from the case of
Egyptian cults on the island of Thera and at Cnidus. The loss
of the Ægean and Asiatic dependencies under Ptolemy III
Euergetes I, with exception of Cyprus, put an end to the spread
of the cult of Sarapis direct from Egypt; it did not, however,
stop the further radiation of this cult to new places from earlier

centres in the Greek world, though the foundation of new centres direct from Alexandria now became rare as a consequence of the strained political situation. By the middle of the second century B.C. the cults of Isis and Sarapis at Athens were held in public; the latter had a temple there north of the Acropolis, the former even appears several times on Athenian coins.

When in 30 B.C. the Mediterranean was united under Roman rule the whole of Greece was permeated with the cult of Sarapis and Isis. The northernmost outpost of Sarapis in the then known world seems to have been at Dionysopolis on the Black Sea; Agathocles had introduced Sarapis to Sicily and since the second century Egyptian cults had existed in various cities in southern Italy. In Rome the cult of Osiris and the existence of his priests is attested in the time of Sulla, but four times between 58 and 48 B.C. attempts were made to repress the Egyptian cults and there was a definite reluctance on the part of Augustus and Tiberius to admit Isis, who had been the goddess of Augustus' enemy, Cleopatra, to Rome.

In 21 B.C. Agrippa launched a kind of Five-Mile Act against the cult of Isis and other Egyptian deities, whose worship within a thousand paces of the city was forbidden. It was not until the time of Caligula that a temple was built to Isis on the Camp of Mars near Rome. Under Vespasian Isis and Sarapis even appeared on imperial coins and Domitian enlarged the temple of *Isis Campensis*, as she was called. At last Caracalla built her a temple on the Quirinalis in the city itself. This advance of Sarapis and Isis westwards was preceded, accompanied or followed by that of other Oriental deities, especially the Syrian ones (*Magna Mater*), but Isis and Sarapis were the only ones whose worship lasted and flourished till the end of paganism. There was hardly any place in the Roman Empire which they had not reached, brought by merchants, officials, slaves and above all soldiers, who frequently changed garrisons and carried with them the religion of their native country or of the country where they had been previously stationed. There was a sanctuary of Isis within the present London area.

During their long and victorious progress through the Roman Empire the Egyptian gods lost much of their original native character. On the other hand they received many features which had been foreign to them, through being identified with many Greek and other gods and goddesses and undergoing interpretations in the light of various philosophical schools by the erudite and educated classes. In the third century A.D. Sarapis became almost a sun-god, and Isis a goddess of the earth, a process which had already started at the end of the first century. In the case of Sarapis it was fostered by the efforts of the emperors to introduce a uniform solar religion throughout the Empire. In Rome Isis was also a patron of sailors and travellers; one of her festivals was held there every year on 5th March, and was called the "Navigation of Isis" (*navigium Isidis*); during this festival a statue of Isis in a boat was driven on a car through the streets—very much as the Egyptian gods used to be in their native country, except that a car was substituted for the shoulders of the "pure ones". This car carrying the boat (*carrus navalis*) was probably passed on to the "carnivals" of the Middle Ages; it thus survived the Isis festivals, the last of which seems to have been celebrated in A.D. 394, though the cult of the goddess lasted till the fifth century.

Attempts have often been made to account for the popularity of Egyptian and other Oriental gods in all countries of the Roman Empire. It has been suggested that since the Egyptian deities were themselves reflections of human beings and their troubles, they made a greater appeal to men than the somewhat cold and bloodless gods of the Greek and Roman pantheon. There can, however, be hardly any doubt that fashion, their strange appearance and character, and the mystery in which these gods were wrapped also played a great part, perhaps, indeed, the greatest. In addition to all this, the perturbing question of what kind of existence, if any, would follow death, was answered by the Egyptian religion by a reassuring promise of eternal happiness in an after-life provided it had been deserved by exemplary conduct during earthly life. Thus the Egyptian religion disposed of a very important human problem for which the Greek and Roman religion and philosophy of the period could offer only a vague and gloomy solution. Minucius Felix, who wrote in about the middle of the second century A.D., could say with complete justification that "these vain deities formerly Egyptian were now also Roman".

The priesthood of the Egyptian gods in the later Empire seems to have been composed mostly of professionals, and a number among them were of Egyptian origin. One of them, a certain Harnuphis, who together with a Roman citizen set up an altar to Isis at Aquileia, the Roman headquarters in the Marcoman wars, even accompanied the Roman Army in the official position of priest. It was to his intercession with the god Hermes Aërios ("Hermes of the Air") that the miraculous rain was ascribed which saved a detachment of Marcus Aurelius' army in A.D. 174 from death by thirst in the territory of Quads and from encirclement and destruction by the enemy. In the inscription of the altar at Aquileia Harnuphis is called "Egyptian scholar" and his Hermes Aërios is a Greek name for the old Egyptian god of the air, Show.

Meanwhile the religious development in Egypt itself went its own way, and here too in the long run the Egyptian gods gained a victory over the Greek ones. The Egyptians found that their gods, together with their language and inherited customs, were the best means of preserving their national character. They did not oppose the spread of the worship of Sarapis, and while the Greeks in Egypt paid homage to Sarapis in the endeavour to please the ruler, who was the sponsor of his cult, and thus to obtain posts in the army and administration, the Egyptians themselves had no objection to the new god since they saw in him their own Osiris-Apis.

At the time of Aelius Aristides the Rhetor (about A.D. 150) no less than forty-two Serapeums are reported from Egypt, which probably means that each nome, the total of which was forty-two, had its own centre of the Sarapis cult. He is invariably called Usar-Hape in all documents written in the Egyptian language, nor is he the only god whose name appears solely in the Egyptian form. Indeed, it may be said with confidence that in no case does the name of a Greek god occur in Egyptian texts, though proper names derived from the names of Greek deities, such as Apollonios, Dionys(i)os, Asklepiades, Hermias or Hierax ("Falcon", the sacred animal of Horus) became current among the Egyptians. Such proper names are not excluded from Egyptian texts, but even then they are often translated, that is, the name of the corresponding Egyptian god is substituted for the Greek in proper names (Hor for Apollonios, Pakhom for Hierax). The Greeks acted slightly less rigidly in this respect, but the Egyptian names of gods do occur now and then in Greek documents, and the names of Osiris, Isis, Horus and Anubis are only seldom replaced by their Greek equivalents. For Suchos (Egyptian Subek) the Greeks had no corresponding god to offer, nor could they parallel the sage Amenothes, Hapu's son, whose healing powers are described with admiration and gratitude in an early Greek ostracon from Thebes. The deities, however, who shared a sanctuary at Der el-Bahari with Amenothes were, according to Greek graffiti left there by visitors, Asklepios and the goddess of health Hygieia. Asklepios is the deified vizier Imhotep; Hygieia, who was Asklepios' daughter in Greek mythology, must here be Hathor.

The contemporary documents, therefore, show clearly that the Greek gods had made little impression on the Egyptians, while the Greeks gradually adopted the native gods, especially where they lived in relatively small numbers among the mass of the Egyptian population. The turning point seems to be 217 b.c., the year of the battle at Raphia (in southern Palestine) and from then onwards we see a steady increase in the prestige of the native religion. Ptolemy IV Philopator, who was reigning at this time, had no longer sufficient numbers of Greeks to form a strong army and was forced to start rearming the Egyptians, a step which the earlier Ptolemies would never have contemplated. A strong contingent of Egyptians fought at Raphia and contributed considerably to the victory, and this, as well as the possession of arms, raised the self-confidence of the Egyptians, who resorted to local insurrections against the Ptolemaic rule. Upper Egypt, in particular, was almost continually in rebellion, and native Egyptian kings maintained themselves independently at Thebes for nineteen years in the latter part of the reign of Ptolemy IV. Important posts both in the army and the administration were also opened to Egyptians. In addition to this, dynastic strife was frequent in the last century and a half of Ptolemaic rule, and in these struggles the kings sought more and more, by according considerable privileges to the temples, to secure the support of the Egyptian priesthood, who exercised great influence over the native population.

This tendency reached its highest point when Ptolemy IX Euergetes II, in his efforts to stop the disorders in the family, decided to rely chiefly upon native support. He decreed far-reaching concessions to the Egyptian temples, especially the cancellation of all arrears of taxes, the burial at state expense of sacred bulls, and the confirmation of the right of asylum to all those temples which had possessed it hitherto. His successors, especially Ptolemy XI Alexander I, granted the right of asylum (*asylia*) to many new temples, thus considerably adding to their power, since this right enabled them to resist the royal administration. It was usually a Greek who acted as guarantor and supported the application by the temple for the asylia, a sign of how intimately connected with Egyptian temples and religion the Greeks had become by the beginning of the first century B.C.

There were no large Greek temples except at Alexandria, and this fact certainly contributed to the Egyptianization of the Greeks in religious matters. The Greeks were in a minority throughout the country, except in Alexandria and the two cities modelled on the Greek city-states, Naucratis in the Delta and Ptolemais in Upper Egypt; their numbers probably hardly exceeded one-fifth of the population anywhere, their temples were scarcely more than modest shrines, while Egyptian deities were housed in imposing buildings, to which a considerable number were added under Ptolemaic rule. In fact the largest and best preserved Egyptian temples date from this period, replacing earlier constructions of Pharaonic times. The temple of Hathor (Aphrodite) at Denderah was begun under Ptolemy XIII Neos Dionysos, under whom the temple of Horus (Apollo) at Edfu begun in 237 B.C. by Ptolemy III Euergetes I, was finished. The earliest decorations of the temple of Subek (Suchos) and Har-wer ("Horus the Elder", Haroëris) at Kom Ombo (ancient Omboi) date from the reign of Ptolemy VI Philometor, so that the construction itself must have been finished by that time. The temples at Erment, that of Khnum and his associate deities at Esna, the temple of Haroëris at Kus and that of Mont and his sacred bull at Medamud, north of Thebes, all date from the period of the Ptolemies. The two limestone temples of the goddess Tripet (Triphis) at Athribis (near Sohâg in Middle Egypt) were built by Ptolemy IX and Ptolemy XIII Auletes respectively. The temple of Isis and her son Harpokrates on the island of Philae were built by Ptolemy II and III, the temple of Hathor at the same place by Ptolemy VI and IX, the sanctuary of Har-hems-nufe (Harensnuphis) by Ptolemy IV and V, and that of Imhotep by Ptolemy II.

The innumerable reliefs and inscriptions which cover the walls of these temples contain no new ideas; they are copies of old religious books which the priests had discovered in temple libraries and now reproduced in stone, changing hardly more than the orthography of the texts and the style of the figures. Thus though all these representations form a valuable source for the study of the earlier stages of the Egyptian religion, they teach us nothing about the religion of the Graeco-Roman period. Nor does this period contribute any original piece of funerary literature, that peculiar kind of religious literature produced for the benefit of the dead. A *Book of Breathings* made its appearance in Thebes in the first century B.C. and the *Book of Traversing Eternity* is of about the same date, but both are nothing more than compilations of phrases extracted from earlier funerary literature without any attempt at originality.

The outstanding characteristic of the late Egyptian religion is the revival and extensive growth of the worship of animals. The cause of it was, to a great extent, the endeavour of the priests and theologians to revert to the archaic state of the Egyptian way of life and thought. They must have known that the cult of animals formed so early a stage in their religion that even at the very beginning of historical times only the remains of it were preserved; but this, more than any other, was the respect in which the Egyptian religion differed outwardly from other religions, so that by laying a special stress on it they might hope to check the influence of other religions, especially the Greek, upon their own. The worship of animals appealed strongly to the mind of the Egyptian fellah, who was in constant contact with animals and nature, and in the Graeco-Roman period this cult grew and was practised with fanaticism.

Diodorus reports that "whoever intentionally killed one of these animals was put to death", but that if he killed a cat or an ibis, whether intentionally or not, he was lynched by gathering crowds without a trial. He himself saw a Roman citizen who had killed a cat by accident punished in this way despite the efforts of the authorities, who were afraid of the anger of Rome, to save the man. The great variety of sacred animals caused much jealousy and hostility, as one animal was worshipped at one place and held in disrespect at another; the bloodthirsty fighting between the two Upper Egyptian towns, Ombos and Tentyra, over their respective sacred animals, described by Juvenal in his well-known fifteenth satire, was certainly not invented but an actual case. Surprisingly enough the Greeks, when adopting native deities, even included sacred animals among them, the crocodile of Suchos being the principal one, since he was sacred in the Fayyum resettled by Egyptians and Greeks under Ptolemy II Philadelphus. The attitude of the philosophically minded among the Greeks is, however, exemplified by that Greek inscription of a first century A.D. vase from Akhmîm (ancient Panopolis): "Having made figures of Osiris and Isis, human or animal faced gods, out of perishable matter, they call them gods. It is stupid to create him who has created you. The bodiless, invisible, inconceivable and immaterial nature it is impossible for a sculptor to represent. In fact it is with intellect and not with hands that it is possible to grasp the divine. There is one temple only of the divine, namely the world."

The adoption of aspects of great gods as minor local deities, examples of which could be seen on the west bank of Thebes during the New Kingdom, is noticeable again in the Graeco-Roman period. Thus the god Subek (Suchos) in the Fayyum, whose worship was centred in the capital of the region, the town of Crocodilopolis, gave origin to various local Subeks in the neighbouring towns and villages: Soknopaios ("Subek, Lord of the Island"), Seknebtynis ("Subek of the town of Tebtynis"), Soknebchunis ("Subek, Lord of Bekhune"), etc. These local differences, which the native rulers had tended to assuage and eliminate in the interest of the internal peace of the country, played into the hands of the authorities since they prevented the Egyptians from forming a united front against the foreign rule.

The danger of Greek cultural supremacy and of the impact

J

of Greek thought continued when Egypt was conquered by
Octavianus in 30 B.C. and the Greeks who were settled in Egypt
succeeded in keeping the status of a ruling minority. Except in
politics the influence of Rome was negligible; Roman sympathies
were on the side of the Greeks, it is true, because of the strong
cultural ties between Rome and Greece, but they had no
further interest in supporting one racial element in the country
against the other. Roman interests in Egypt were of a purely
material nature and were best served by a certain equilibrium
in the country. To the Egyptians the Roman conquest meant
no more than the passage from one foreign rule to another, and
they recognized the divine nature of the Roman emperor with
the same readiness with which they had conferred it on a king
of Macedonian origin. But their conception of kingship could
not fail to exercise a strong influence throughout the empire
and encouraged the swift rise of the Roman emperor to the
status of a divine ruler.

The conquest of Egypt by Christianity started as early as
the first century A.D. Practically nothing is known about the
beginnings of the Christian community there; contemporary
documents cast no light on it. It seems certain that Christianity
came through Alexandria, whither it had been brought from
Jerusalem by relatives and friends of the powerful community
of Alexandrian Jews living there. In Palestine the movement
had started with the sole aim of a spiritual rebirth of the chosen
people and of preparing them for the end of the existing world
order and the coming of the kingdom of heaven. It, therefore,
lacked any interest in acquiring adepts outside Judaism, and
this is certainly responsible for the very slow initial rise of
Christianity. Other religions paid very little attention to it and
public opinion confused Christians with Jews. It was only
gradually that interest in the Christian religion asserted itself
among the Gentiles, and it came about spontaneously without
any proselytism on the part of the Christians. St. Paul,
himself a convert, set out on a missionary journey, but even he
preached first in synagogues.

The rejection of Christian ideas by official Judaism eventually broke the link between Christians and Jews and also turned
the attention of the Christians beyond the Jewish people, to

mankind in general. Judging from the later history of the Christian church in Egypt, when the Egyptians were invariably in opposition to the capital of the Empire, and backed the dogma declared heretical by Rome or Constantinople, one cannot avoid the impression that defiance of the Roman authorities largely fostered the spread of Christianity in Egypt in the first centuries of our era. For though other religions showed no hostility to Christians, these were definitely looked on with disfavour by the Roman authorities and persecuted by them at irregular intervals.

The reason for this attitude on the part of the secular power was the intransigent character of Christian monotheism, which refused to recognize or admit that the emperor was a god and to acquiesce in the worship of the state. The early Christians, whose minds were firmly fixed on the promised coming of the kingdom of God, could not but regard the existing order with contempt and look upon it as quite temporary; the great majority of the very early Christians probably lived in the faith that the return of the Saviour was going to take place in their lifetime. The worldly authorities thought this behaviour subversive and tried by the exercise of police measures to stop such a revolutionary movement, but in vain. This persecution could not fail to increase the appeal which Christianity had for the large mass of the Egyptian population suffering from the heavy taxation introduced by the Ptolemies and pitilessly exploited by the Roman government. The struggle against the secular authorities led at last to the struggle against the other recognized religions, Egyptian, Greek and Oriental alike.

Attempts have sometimes been made to show that among early Christian beliefs there are traces of the influence of the Egyptian religion. A direct influence can hardly be proved; it is, however, extremely likely that the Egyptian religion had its share in the formation of a common cultural background and the fertile soil from which Christianity rose and spread. In fact, neither the beliefs nor the requirements which Christianity imposed upon its devotees lacked analogies in contemporary religions and philosophical thought. That good conduct was indispensable for joining God and for happiness in the hereafter was an idea which is first met with in Egypt as early as the end of the third millenium B.C., and the Egyptian literature of wisdom also teaches that right conduct is the best guarantee of happiness in this world. The requirement of ritual purity and the change of the latter into moral purity was current. The Egyptian, together with all ancient religions had arrived at the idea that all different gods are in the end only one God, the Father who loves man, his creation, and directs him according to His will. The resurrection of Jesus had its exact parallel in Osiris.

On the other hand Christianity added much that was new, which made it popular especially with the lower classes among whom it was already widely spread at a time when the upper classes, the wealthy and intellectuals, still adhered to paganism: the requirement of love for fellow Christians, disinterest in worldly riches and power, generosity towards the poor, mutual support among the members of the Christian community, all helped to create or increase the sense of security among the poor, the humble and the slaves. Above all, there was the promise of God's grace, which would enable the believer to live up to the requirements of his faith, and instead of a mere divine direction of world affairs there was a direct divine intervention to change the existing unsatisfactory state of things for the better. The death of God, instead of being a momentary incident in the struggle of good and evil, assumed a more appealing motive, the redemption of man, thus raising the importance of man to an unprecedented height.

It cannot, however, be denied that when greater numbers were gained for the Christian faith, various pagan elements found their way into Christian beliefs and religious practices. The worship of the Virgin Mary and the picture of her with the child Jesus in her arms almost certainly owe a great deal to the influence of the goddess Isis with the young Horus on her lap. The creation of various local saints, the erection of their shrines, pilgrimages to these holy places and festivals around them were substitutes—almost the continuation—of the worship of former local deities. The resemblance between St. George killing the dragon with his spear to Horus killing his enemy, the evil god Sētekh, in the form of a crocodile, must be very striking to anyone. Even the choice of 25th December for the date of the birth of Jesus and the celebration of Christmas perpetuated the old solar festival of the "birth of Rē" (Egn. Mesorē). The practice of astrology and magic which had long been forbidden was now tolerated and countless magical texts have come down to us from Christian Egypt. They resemble the pagan ones except that the names of the old Egyptian gods are replaced by those of Jesus and the saints, who are even threatened if they should not comply with the magician's orders.

By the end of the second century there was a flourishing Christian school at Alexandria, and Lower Egypt was covered with a dense network of Christian communities. It is interesting that the oldest manuscript of the Gospels on papyrus comes from Egypt; its date is the first half of the second century; it is a fragment of St. John, chap. xviii, now at Manchester. Half a century later a fierce persecution of Christians broke out, under Decius (A.D. 249–251), but this was only the vain struggle of a pagan minority against the overwhelming Christian majority which existed by that time even in Upper Egypt. This is clearly shown by the fact that the name of Decius, who sponsored the persecution, is the last emperor's name to occur in hieroglyphic writing on the walls of an Egyptian pagan temple, that of the god Khnum at Esna. Soon after Gallienus (A.D. 260–268) a measure of religious toleration was granted to Christians, and at the end of the third century and the beginning of the fourth everything goes to witness the complete victory of Christianity over the Egyptian religion. The last persecution took place in the year 303 under Diocletian, but the last known hieroglyphic inscription on a stela from Erment (now in the British Museum) is of a slightly earlier date: A.D. 295, the year of Diocletian's joint reign with his co-rulers Maximianus and Valerius. It represents the emperor making offerings to the sacred bull, Buchis, which died in that year when "his soul (*bai*) flew up to heaven", probably the very last Buchis in existence. From then onwards Greek and the native Egyptian language, called Coptic, a deformation of Aiguptiakos (Egyptian) and written in Greek letters were the only vehicles of written thought in the country. It was into Coptic that the Bible was translated at about that time for the use of the Egyptian population, and a complete break was made with the old pagan literature.

At about the end of the third century the first hermit, St. Anthony, appeared in the desert mountains east of Aphroditopolis. In A.D. 313 Constantine the Great and Licinius proclaimed the equality of all religions in their Milan edict, and after this pagans were on the defensive in many parts of the Roman world, including Egypt. They were attacked in various places by Christians whose intolerance was directed indiscriminately against all pagan religions. From equality it was only a step to the first restrictions under Constantius (A.D. 337–361); and finally under Theodosius (A.D. 379–395) Christianity was declared the official religion of the empire and pagan cults were forbidden altogether. Fanatical Christian mobs set themselves to destroy the pagan temples, though the emperor's orders were to preserve them as works of art and to turn them into administrative buildings wherever possible.

But paganism lingered on for another century. In A.D. 415 the female philosopher, Hypatia, was stoned to death at Alexandria, though enlightened Christians such as Synesius, Bishop of Cyrenaica, were her friends. It was only far away in the south, on the frontier between Egypt and Nubia, that a small pagan community could continue to worship at the temple of Isis on the little island of Philae, protected by the redoubtable Blemmyes in neighbouring Nubia. In 451, after a long series of invasions into Egypt, the Blemmyes concluded a treaty with the Emperor Marcian's commander, Florus, the clauses of which guaranteed to their priests access to Philae and the right of bringing sacrifices to Isis. The Blemmyes were fervent worshippers of Isis and were regularly allowed to borrow the sacred statue of the goddess from the island. Blemmyan visitors left graffiti written in Greek and Demotic, the contemporary pagan Egyptian script, on the walls of the temple side by side with those of the local Egyptian priests. Two of the latter, Esmet the Elder and Esmet the Younger, are the last who are known through their Demotic inscription of A.D. 452. In the middle of the sixth century, when the treaty with the Blemmyes had been in force for a hundred years, Justinian at last succeeded in closing the temple of Isis; he threw her priests into prison and brought the statues of the gods of Philae to Constantinople. By that time Nubia herself had been completely christianized.

BIBLIOGRAPHY

The following list of more recent works on Egyptian religion is neither exhaustive nor is it intended to justify the statements made in the present book. Its sole purpose is to serve as a starting point to the readers who might desire more detailed information on the subject.

Breasted, James H., *Development of Religion and Thought in Ancient Egypt*, London, 1912.

Röder, Günther, *Urkunden zur Religion des alten Ägypten*, Jena, 1915.

Boylan, Patrick, *Thoth, the Hermes of Egypt*, London, 1922.

Max Müller, W., *Egyptian Mythology*, New Hampshire, U.S.A., 1918; London, 1924.

Bonnet, H., *Ägyptische Religion*, Leipzig-Erlangen 1924 (in *Bilderatlas zur Religionsgeschichte*, edited by D. H. Haas).

Kees, Hermann, *Totenglauben und Jenseitsvorstellungen der alten Ägypter*, Leipzig, 1926.

Sethe, Kurt, *Urgeschichte und älteste Religion der Ägypter*, Leipzig, 1930.

Shorter, Alan W., *An Introduction to Egyptian Religion*, London, 1931.

Budge, Sir E. A. Wallis, *From Fetish to God in Ancient Egypt*, London, 1934.

Erman, Adolf, *Die Religion der Ägypter*, Berlin and Leipzig 1934; French translation *La religion des Égyptiens*, by H. Wild, Paris, 1937.

Shorter, Alan W., *The Egyptian Gods*, London, 1937.

Breasted, James H., *The Dawn of Conscience*, London, 1939.

Kees, Hermann, *Der Götterglaube im alten Ägypten*, Leipzig, 1941.

Mercer, Samuel A. B., *Horus, Royal God of Egypt*, Grafton (Mass., U.S.A.), 1942.

Drioton, É., *La religion égyptienne dans ses grandes lignes*, Cairo, 1945.

Sandman Holmberg, Maj, *The God Ptah*, Lund, 1946.

Jéquier, Gustave, *Considérations sur les religions égyptiennes*, Neuchâtel, 1946.

Desroches-Noblecourt, C., *Les religions égyptiennes*, in: L'histoire générale des religions, pp. 205–331, Paris, 1947.

Sainte Fare Garnot, Jean, *La vie religieuse dans l'ancienne Égypte*, Paris, 1948.

Frankfort, Henri, *Ancient Egyptian Religion, an Interpretation*, New York, 1948.

Junker, Hermann, *Pyramidenzeit, Das Wesen der altägyptischen Religion*, Einsiedeln (Switzerland), 1949.

Mercer, Samuel, A. B., *The Religion of Ancient Egypt*, London, 1949.

Vandier, Jacques, *La religion égyptienne*, Édition "Mana", 2nd ed., Paris, 1949.

Murray, Margaret A., *Egyptian Religious Poetry*, London, 1949.

Bonnet, H., *Reallexikon der ägyptischen Religionsgeschichte*, Berlin, 1952.

Bell, H. Idris, *Cults and Creeds in Graeco-roman Egypt*, Liverpool, 1954.

INDEX

A.—author; D.—deity; K.—king; L.—locality; P.—private person; Q.—queen.

A

Abusimbel, L., 130
Abusîr, L., 70, 112
Abydos, L., 22, 26, 36, 59, 87, 101, 105, 106, 107, 121
Aegean (islands), 138
Aelius Aristides, A., 141
Africa, North, 15
Agamemnon, 136
Agathocles, 139
Agrippa, 139
Aha, D., 72
Akhet, D., 58
Akhetaton, L., 63, 66
Akhmîm, L., 145
Alexander the Great, K., 48, 129, 136
Alexandria, L., 136, 137, 139, 143, 146, 149, 150
Amarna, L., 63, 69
Amasis, K., 134
Amaunet, D., 37, 42
Amduat, 95
Amenemhet (I), K., 37
Amenemope, a builder, 126
—— A., 77
Amenhotep (I), K. and D., 73
—— II, K., 126
—— III, K., 49, 62, 110, 126-7, 128, 130
—— IV, K., 61, 62, 63, 127
—— Hapu's son, D., 49
Amenothes Paapios, D., 49, 142
Amente, 80
Amentet, D., 59, 80
Ammon, D., 135, 138
Amon-Rē, D., 38, 61, 62, 69, 70, 131
Amun, D., 25, 30, 37, 38, 42, 53, 61, 62, 63, 66, 69, 70, 73, 75, 101, 117, 118, 119, 120, 121, 128, 129, 130, 131, 132, 133, 134, 135
Anat, D., 126, 127, 128, 129, 135
Andjeti, D., 35

Aniba, L., 130
Anpet, L., 25
anthropomorphization of gods, 27-9
Antinoupolis, L., 24, 31
Anubis, D., 20, 22, 27, 29, 60, 61, 89, 105, 131, 136, 142
Anuket, D., 130
Anupew, D., 22
Anyt, D., 127
Aphrodite, D., 127, 134, 135, 143
Aphroditopolis, L., 23, 150
Apis, D., 24, 136, 137, 138
Apollo, D., 134, 135, 143
Apollonios, P., 141, 142
Aquileia, L., 141
Arabian desert, 13
Ares, D., 135
Armant (Erment), L., 37, 143, 149
Artemis, D., 135
Ash, D., 28, 124
Ashima, D., 135
Ashmunein, L., 24
Asia, 15, 38, 47, 125, 127, 128, 129, 133, 134, 136, 137
Asklepiades, 141
Asklepios, D., 50, 142
Assurbanipal, K., 132
Assyria, 128, 132
Astarte, D., 47, 126, 127, 128, 129
Astartieion, a sanctuary, 129
Athene, D., 135
Athens, L., 138, 139
Athribis, L., 23, 144
Aton, D., 62, 63, 64, 65, 66
atonism, 69
Atum, D., 30, 43, 44, 46, 52
Augustus, emperor, 139

B

Ba'al, D., 126, 127
Ba'alat, D., 126, 127
Ba'al-zephon, D., 127